The Economics of Non-selfish Behaviour

The Economics of Non-selfish Behaviour

Decisions to Contribute Money to Public Goods

Stephan Meier

Research Center for Behavioral Economics and Decision-Making, Federal Reserve Bank of Boston; and Harvard University, USA

Edward Elgar
Cheltenham, UK • Northampton, MA, USA.

Published by
Edward Elgar Publishing Limited
Glensanda House
Montpellier Parade
Cheltenham
Glos GL50 1UA
UK

Edward Elgar Publishing, Inc.
136 West Street
Suite 202
Northampton
Massachusetts 01060
USA

A catalogue record for this book
is available from the British Library

Library of Congress Cataloguing in Publication Data

Meier, Stephan, 1972–
    The economics of non-selfish behaviour : decisions to contribute money to public goods / Stephan Meier.
        p.cm.
    Includes bibliographical references.
    1. Altruism–Economic aspects. 2. Helping behavior–Economics aspects. 3. Public goods. 4. Charity. I. Title.

HM1146.M45 2005
302.1'4–dc22

2005049467

ISBN-13: 978 1 84542 441 1
ISBN-10: 1 84542 441 7

Printed and bound in Great Britain by MPG Books Ltd, Bodmin, Cornwall

Contents

Acknowledgements   vi
Preface   vii

1   Introduction   1

PART I: THEORETICAL CONSIDERATIONS

2   A Survey of Economic Theories on Pro-social Behaviour   9

PART II: EMPIRICAL ANALYSIS

3   Pro-social Behaviour in a Natural Laboratory   53

4   Social Comparisons and Pro-social Behaviour: A Field Experiment   79

5   Matching Donations: Subsidizing Pro-social Behaviour   99

6   Economic Education and Pro-social Behaviour: Selection or   114
     Indoctrination?

7   Concluding Remarks   135

References   141
Index   163

Acknowledgements

This book is based on my research undertaken at the Institute for Empirical Research in Economics at the University of Zurich. The views expressed herein are solely those of the author and not those of the Federal Reserve System or the Federal Reserve Bank of Boston. I want especially to thank my mentor Prof. Dr. Dr. h.c. mult. Bruno S. Frey for giving me an apprenticeship in economics. He supported, challenged and inspired me to analyse the world from an economic perspective while always being open to the limits of economic theory and to insights from other social sciences. The ideas presented in this book, which were developed in many discussions and joint research projects, represent this broad understanding of economics. He created an atmosphere within his group from which I have greatly benefited. Many conversations with Dr. Matthias Benz, Dr. Lorenz Götte, Reto Jegen, Dr. Marcel Kucher, Simon Lüchinger and Dr. Alois Stutzer have influenced my thinking and the content of this book. I am particularly grateful to Matthias Benz, Lorenz Götte, Simon Lüchinger and Alois Stutzer for the care with which they read earlier drafts of this study. I wish to thank Prof. Dr. Simon Gächter, with whom I discussed the ideas presented in this book. I greatly profited from the conversations with him.

I thank the administration of the University of Zurich for giving me access without bureaucratic red tape to a unique data set. A special thanks goes to Thomas Tschümperlin, who made the field experiments possible. I also want to thank Rosemary Brown and Dr. Misha Kavka, who helped me to improve my English-language skills and subsequently the syntax in this book. Sarah and Mic Frédérickx (-Milic) helped me with the English and computer crashes.

Finally, I want to thank Elisabeth Glas for supporting me throughout the whole process in every aspect. She read parts of the manuscript, helped me with the layout and was never tired of listening to the preliminary ideas and results of my research. Special thanks also to my parents, to whom this book is dedicated.

Preface

The tsunami catastrophe that hit a number of East-Asian countries on 24 December 2005 cost the lives of about 250,000 persons. It gave rise to unprecedented donations from governments, but more importantly also from private individuals. In Switzerland, a country of only 7.5 million people, for example, 130 million Swiss Francs (about 100 million Euros) were collected within a few days. This demonstrates the importance of pro-social behaviour under the specific condition of a murderous sea wave. At the same time, there are many people, especially children, starving to death in many countries, where such pro-social behaviour is not being awakened. The stark differences in private donations according to the conditions obtaining makes it an important task for us to understand better what motivates people to donate.

In this book Stephan Meier presents a fascinating, empirically based analysis of donations. He uses a unique data set of the behaviour of Zurich students for the purpose of testing pro-social behaviour. The data are composed of a huge number of observations with a panel structure, which presents a rare opportunity for an in-depth analysis. The author presents one of the first systematic tests of giving behaviour outside the laboratory by using the natural experimental method. The whole work, ranging from careful data collection, setting up the experiment, to estimating with advanced econometric estimation techniques, is performed very well indeed. The book seeks to answer two specific questions:

1. When do people contribute to public goods?
2. What determines pro-social behaviour?

Stephan Meier seeks to understand not only the extent of pro-social behaviour, in particular giving money and working time, but he also makes a great effort to understand in depth the motivation underlying such behaviour. He understands pro-social behaviour to be all behaviour systematically deviating from narrow material self-interest. A great number of influences are taken into account and care is taken to isolate the different effects from each other. To reach this goal the author skilfully combines field and laboratory evidence.

The book is able to explain a large share of individual giving, which is not possible with standard economic theory, based on the narrow self-interest hypothesis. Stephan Meier convincingly documents that people do contribute to public goods, often in sizeable amounts. In particular, he makes the following significant contributions to economic knowledge:

- People do not free-ride on the contributions of others.
- People systematically respond to relative price changes in the form of monetary incentives to giving.
- The interactions between individuals and groups are relevant.
- Education influences giving, but economics training does not make students more selfish but rather there is a selection effect, at least in the case of business economics students.
- Institutions strongly affect pro-social behaviour, an aspect which tends to be treated lightly, or is even disregarded, in behavioural economics.

Stephan Meier concludes that the prospect of people behaving pro-socially is not as gloomy as often predicted by economic theory, but the probability and extent of such pro-social behaviour strongly depends on institutional conditions. He emphasizes that contributions to public goods are possible without government intervention. Rather, institutions need to be designed to foster pro-social behaviour. In particular, the procedures must be perceived to be fair. Giving behaviour is also conditional on the behaviour of others. Institutions must avoid fostering low expectations about the behaviour of others in order to increase pro-social behaviour. People tend to underestimate the extent of pro-social behaviour in a group. Therefore, social interaction tends to increase pro-social behaviour. He also finds that matching donations support pro-social behaviour.

Bruno S. Frey
University of Zurich and CREMA – Center for Research on Economics, Management and the Arts

January 2005

1. Introduction

Shortly after Christmas 2003, an earthquake hit the region surrounding the Iranian city of Bam. The natural disaster killed more than 40,000 people and left many more with nothing but the clothes they were wearing. International aid was quick to arrive. All over the world, people donated money to help the Iranians. Governments approved large aid packages containing food, shelter tents and rescue troops. For example, the donation campaign in Switzerland was able to raise over 9 million Swiss Francs from individual donors in less than two months (in addition to aid financed through tax money).

The large amount donated to Iran from all over the world is surprising in three senses. Firstly, not only are economists probably astonished by the fact that a large number of people are willing to give money away, but standard economic theory, which relies on a narrow self-interest hypothesis, is obviously not a useful guide in explaining these anonymous donations. According to this theory, people only care about their own utility and therefore do not help others; even if people were to care about the Iranian population, individuals would free-ride on the contributions of others, with a result of close to no contributions. But, obviously, people do seem to care for others. Secondly, it is particularly surprising that money has been donated to the Iranian population. As an Islamic theocracy, reluctant to follow so-called Western values such as basic human rights and democratic rules, Iran can hardly be called a 'friend' whom one wants to support. But even the US population spent large amounts of money to support the population of their erstwhile enemy number 1. Thirdly, additional motives for helping others have difficulty in explaining the anonymous donations. It is, for example, hard to imagine that the poor people of Iran will be able to reciprocate in kind to help victims of a future earthquake in the USA.

This is just one example where individuals donate money in large sums. Economics needs to address and to explain these phenomena. The level of donations, however, is only of limited interest in the quest to understand pro-social behaviour. The marginal effects are much more informative. The interesting question is therefore not whether people behave pro-socially at all, but under what circumstances people's pro-social behaviour is (marginally) more pronounced. If these conditions can be isolated, it will be possible to infer the underlying motives for contributing to a good cause. One can, for example, compare the donations by the Swiss populace to Iran with Swiss donations to victims of a landslide in the canton of Wallis in 2000. The amount of donations received to help their relatively wealthy fellow citizens was around eightfold the donations to the Iranians (74 million Swiss Francs). The large difference in donations between these very similar situations, that is aid to people affected by a natural disaster, can give initial interesting insights into the motivation for helping other people. There are at least three differences between the two situations. One explanation of the difference stresses that solidarity and cooperative behaviour is more pronounced within a group (for example, Swiss) than between groups (for example, inhabitants of two nationalities). A second explanation could be the expectations of the donors that, if they were in a situation of emergency themselves, the inhabitants of the canton of Wallis would reciprocate their aid better than the Iranians. A third potential explanation focuses on the different methods for eliciting the donations: while in the case of donations to Wallis, people could phone in and offer their donations on the radio, in the case of donations to Iran no such possibility existed.[1] The offer of donations on the radio can increase the prestige people recoup from charitable giving and at the same time lead to social interaction effects. If people hear that many others are donating, they will also donate.

In order to understand the motivations for behaving pro-socially, one has to distinguish between these potential influences on the variation in pro-social behaviour. However, the comparison between the donations to Iran and those to Wallis cannot be conclusive; too many variables simultaneously influence charitable giving in these cases. As long as the driving forces cannot be isolated from each other, the interpretation is ambiguous.

The aim of this book is to overcome such ambiguities. The reasons for donating money as well as time to a good cause is analysed more systematically – both in theory and empirically. In pursuing this endeavour I define pro-social behaviour in a broader way: pro-social behaviour includes not only donations to charities but all behaviour that deviates systematically from narrow self-interest[2], one of the core tenets of economic theory. By systematic I mean that the deviations are not caused by random errors of individuals seeking to maximize their self-interest but are inherent in human preferences.

According to standard economic theory, people contribute to the public good suboptimally. This leads to gloomy predictions about human behaviour; for example, as the natural environment has characteristics of a public good, people are expected to pollute extensively, while income redistribution ought to be opposed by the expected net-payers, since people should take full advantage of any situation in which they can increase their own utility – even at somebody else's expense. However, in reality such selfish behaviour is observed less often than expected and in many situations people are willing to provide public goods privately. In order to analyse pro-social behaviour, the empirical part of this book focuses on charitable giving by individuals as one form of contributions to public goods.[3] Since we observe that in many situations individuals do not in fact maximize their narrow, material self-interest, the core question of this study is about the conditions that influence pro-social behaviour. If it is possible to isolate the conditions that lead to pro-social behaviour, this will increase the understanding of the motivations to contribute money and time to public goods.

To add insight to the phenomenon of individual decision-making about contributions to public goods, this book pursues two main goals:

1. *To add to the understanding of the conditions under which people contribute to public goods*   Standard economic theory cannot explain pro-social behaviour in a satisfying way, neither its level nor its variance. Therefore, it is necessary to enrich the narrow self-interest hypothesis with insights from other social sciences, especially social psychology. In the survey section, the theoretical approaches to pro-social behaviour are presented and evaluated. The different theories vary substantially in their behavioural predictions and are often mutually exclusive. The survey, therefore, presents empirical evidence to discriminate between the theories by focusing explicitly on field evidence. It will, however, become clear that there are still many open questions about pro-social behaviour.

   In the empirical part of the book, a number of these open questions will be analysed. The empirical results add to the progress of research. Systematic behavioural reactions of people to changing conditions lead to insights about the importance of various theoretical explanations for pro-social behaviour. It is, for example, found that social interaction effects are important for pro-social behaviour. In contrast to predictions made by altruism models, the empirical evidence shows that people do not free-ride on the contributions of others but even increase their charitable giving when observing others do so as well.

   The empirical results presented in this book have important implications for designing institutions that wish to foster pro-social behaviour. These implications will be discussed and evaluated. For example, the result suggesting the importance of social interaction effects implies that individuals' behaviour varies positively with the perceived group average. Avoiding an overestimation of selfish behaviour in a group has policy implications, which will be differentiated and discussed.

2.   *To analyse the variation of pro-social behaviour in natural laboratories*
     For decades, results from laboratory experiments have offered insights
     about motivations for pro-social behaviour. However, it is still unclear
     how these results can be applied outside laboratories. This book aims to
     narrow this gap by analysing pro-social behaviour in the field. The
     empirical tests, therefore, represent one of the first systematic tests of a
     particular question outside the laboratory. For example, there is a
     relatively large discussion and a number of laboratory results available
     on the question of whether teaching the standard model of rational
     choice erodes students' citizenship behaviour. The evidence presented in
     this book is based on the first test systematically to analyse this question
     outside a laboratory setting – and the results deviate from laboratory
     results. The analysis of field data has, however, the disadvantage that
     exogenous variations of the interesting variables are relatively rare. It is
     therefore sometimes not possible to exclude selection effects and to
     make conclusive statements about causality. In the empirical part of the
     book, I avoid these shortcomings by creating exogenous variation in a
     field experiment.

    In order to pursue these two goals the book is divided into two parts and
seven chapters. The first part sets the theoretical stage for the empirical
analysis of the second part. Chapter 2 therefore presents a survey of theories
on pro-social behaviour and discusses the existing empirical evidence. Since
the literature on pro-social behaviour contains an almost countless number of
scientific contributions, the survey orders the arguments and concentrates on
field evidence about pro-social behaviour. At the end of this chapter, open
questions will be formulated to serve as a guide to the empirical part of the
book.
    The second and empirical part of the book tests various theoretical expla-
nations using a data set on the decisions of all students at the University of
Zurich to contribute to two social funds.
    Chapter 3 presents the data set. This is done in three steps. Firstly, the
decision situation is presented. Secondly, a descriptive analysis of the general
giving pattern offers insights about the motivation for contributing to the two
funds. What turns out to be particularly important to the decision to donate is
the context in which the decision is made (for example, framing effects). And
thirdly, the econometric models to be used in the following chapters are
explained and applied to the results of the descriptive analysis. The three
chapters that follow are all based on this data set. Chapter 4 presents the
results of a field experiment which analyses whether students are influenced
by the average behaviour of the student population. Here, the relationship
between individual behaviour and group behaviour can be tested for the first

time in a field experiment. Chapter 5 analyses whether pro-social behaviour responds to a change in relative prices, since for economics the functioning of the relative price effect is crucial. The conditions under which monetary incentives can have detrimental effects for pro-social behaviour are discussed. Chapter 6 discusses whether education and, in particular, economic training, have a negative effect on pro-social behaviour. It is an often heard claim that economics education undermines citizenship behaviour. This claim is here tested using behaviour in a natural setting. Chapter 7 summarizes the results of the study and points to the importance of these outcomes for economic theory and policy.

NOTES

1. Personal contact with the chief of communication of 'Glückskette Schweiz', Roland Jeanneret, 2 February, 2004.
2. The term self-interest is used throughout this book in reference to narrow material self-interest. Of course, if, say, pro-sociality provides utility to individuals, then it is in their best self-interest to behave pro-socially, in the sense that this raises their utility. However, this use does not fit most people's understanding of what self-interest means, that is of material self-interest as opposed to pro-social behaviour.
3. Much literature is devoted to understanding donations between governments (for example, Frey and Schneider, 1986; Alesina and Dollar, 2000). It is clear that the motivation of politicians (for example, the bureaucracy of the USA) to send rescue packages to Iran may be quite different from individuals' motivations. The same can be assumed for the philanthropic acts of corporations (for example, Navarro, 1988).

PART I

Theoretical Considerations

2. A Survey of Economic Theories on Pro-social Behaviour

2.1 BEHAVIOUR BEYOND SELF-INTEREST

The self-interest of individuals leads to favourable outcomes for society. According to one of the most important insights in economics, the pursuit of self-interest by consumers as well as by producers is not only consistent with broader social goals, but is even required by them. This is famously stated by Adam Smith: 'it is not from the benevolence of the butcher, the brewer, or the baker that we expect our dinner, but from their regard of their own interest. We address ourselves not to their humanity, but to their self-love, and never talk to them of our necessities, but of their advantage' (Smith, 1776 [1991]: 20). Thus, individuals need not consciously optimize social welfare; rather, the invisible hand of the market mechanism guides them.

Adam Smith, however, was also aware of the fact that the pursuit of self-interest does not always maximize the 'wealth of nations' and even sometimes falls far short of reaching the socially desired outcome. When the costs and benefits of an action accrue to people other than the decision-maker, the market mechanism can break down. For example, negative external effects are incurred if the decision-maker does not bear the total costs and therefore consumes too much of the good involved. This problem occurs in the well-known 'tragedy of the commons' (Hardin, 1968): people neglect the cost burden they place on others when they decide on the use of common resources. Their self-interest then leads to an overuse of the scarce resources. Conversely, in the case of positive external effects individuals do not consider the benefits for others in their decision calculus and provide too little of the good in question. In the production of art, for example, the market mechanism tends to provide a socially suboptimal amount of culture due to positive externalities (Throsby, 1994; Frey, 2000). The provision of a public good, where an equivalence between people who pay and people who use the good is lacking, illustrates the problem of the pursuit of self-interest clearly: individuals will free-ride on the contributions of others, because they cannot be excluded from using the public good.

The provision of a (linear) pure public good (which is both non-rival and non-excludable) can be analysed in the following way.

Each potential contributor i in the group of n identical persons has an income Y_i, which he or she can either donate to a fund F or use to consume private goods. If d_i is the contribution to the fund, the individual is privately able to consume $Y_i - d_i$. The individual's earning from the fund is a multiple m of the sum of donations from all the participants, $m \sum d_i$.[1] A public good problem exists whenever $1/n < m < 1$. When $m < 1$, it is never optimal for a self-interested person to contribute to the public good because the contribution costs her or him one unit, but gives her or him only m in return. When $m > 1/n$, contributing to the public good is always optimal for the group as a whole, because donating one unit to the public good costs the individual one unit but earns $n*m$ for the group. For a self-interested individual, there is a unique dominant strategy in which all persons in the group *free-ride* (that is, contribute nothing). All public good situations, which are also called social dilemmas, share the same characteristic: individual, self-interested decision-making will lead to a socially suboptimal provision of the public good.

An enormous number of decision situations can be characterized as public good problems. For example, people free-ride on the efforts of others to protect the environment; no consumer puts effort into fighting for reduced tariff rates because everyone profits from the resulting lower prices; people let others organize a community event; too few people donate blood because, if needed, he or she will receive blood anyway; people do not enforce a social norm, for example not to litter in a public park, because they think that others should do it, and so on. All these individual calculations result in suboptimal outcomes: too little environmental protection, no reduction in tariff rates, difficulties in finding somebody to organize community events, too few blood donors, and nobody who enforces social norms. In general, nobody will contribute a sufficient amount of money or time to provide a socially optimal amount of public goods. Based on the analysis that people will not contribute to public goods because it is in their self-interest to free-ride, the collective production of the public good financed by tax money can be seen as a solution to the problem. Free-riding is expected to be minimized, as everybody has to pay taxes. And yet, due to the low probability of getting caught and being penalized, paying taxes is also a public good and people will also try to evade paying taxes in order to pursue their self-interest (e.g. Alm et al., 1992).

In reality, people free-ride less often than is predicted by standard economic theory. People behave in a number of situations not according to narrow self-interest but rather pro-socially: for instance, most people actually pay their taxes, a fact that cannot be explained by relying on strict self-interest axioms (Slemrod, 1992; Andreoni et al., 1998). Tax payment can therefore be considered a 'quasi-voluntary act' (Levi, 1988). Individuals do vote, although due to the low probability of having the decisive vote the expected utility of voting is close to zero and standard economic theory predicts that few people will show up at the ballot boxes (for example, Mueller, 2003). In the political process, voters express their preferences for income redistribution in a way that goes beyond financial self-interest (Pommerehne and Schneider, 1985; Shabman and Stephenson, 1994; Bütler, 2002). Under certain circumstances people are able to prevent the overuse of a common-pool resource (Ostrom, 1990); a large part of the production of open source software is difficult to explain by relying on strict self-interested behaviour (see Osterloh et al., 2003).

According to economic theory, people should take advantage of any opportunity to exploit society or another individual – but they do not. In various situations in the political sphere, in firms or in the family, people are 'rent leavers', meaning that they 'do not invest in something that is unproductive for others but that would increase their own income' (Bohnet and Frey, 1997: 711). Individuals therefore contribute substantial amounts of money and time to public goods. Estimations for the USA show that in 1995, more than 68 per cent of households contributed to charitable organizations. In 1998, these private households donated more than 134 billion USD (Andreoni, 2002). In the same year, more than 50 per cent of all adult Americans did voluntary work, amounting to 5 million full-time equivalents[2] (Anheier and Salamon, 1999: 58). Although the extent of charitable contributions and the engagement in volunteer work is smaller in Europe, it is still substantial: in Europe, on average 32.1 per cent of the population volunteer.[3] Taking the hours volunteered into account, this amounts to 4.5 million full-time equivalent volunteers for the ten European countries taken into consideration (Anheier and Salamon, 1999: 58). The self-interest hypothesis has also been rejected in a large number of laboratory experiments. With respect to contributions to public goods, it has been found that people invest up to between 40 per cent and 60 per cent of their endowment in public goods (for surveys, see, for example, Ledyard, 1995; Camerer and Thaler, 1995; Camerer, 2003). In dictator games, people often voluntarily give part of the money to the recipients. However, there is a large variation, from 0 per cent to 70 per cent, of dictators who give more than nothing, depending on the conditions. For example, if people could donate part of the pie to a charity, more than 70 per cent donated on average 30 per cent of their endowment (Eckel and Grossman, 1996a). A recent study of experimental ultimatum games in 15 societies around the world reveals that 'the canonical model of the self-interested material pay-off maximizing actor is systematically violated' (Henrich et al., 2001: 77).

The overwhelming evidence about contributions to public goods and cooperation in social dilemmas shows that the public good problem is not as severe as assumed by standard economic theory. People are in fact not solely concerned with their self-interest. As a result of these findings, a large number of theories have evolved to explain people's pro-social behaviour and the variation in their respective behaviour. This chapter surveys these various economic theories of pro-social behaviour. In each subsection, one specific theory is investigated and predictions for behaviour are derived. The hypotheses are then tested against existing empirical evidence on pro-social behaviour. The empirical findings presented are mainly based on field and survey evidence rather than on laboratory experiments, but laboratory studies are also referred to where appropriate. Fehr and Schmidt (2003), Camerer (2003) and Konow (2003b) offer good surveys of theories of fairness and reciprocity with a focus on experiments. For at least two decades, laboratory experiments have challenged the standard economic assumption. While experimental research leads to many insights about the fundamentals of human behaviour, it is still unclear exactly how these results can be generalized outside the laboratory situation. This overview and the field evidence presented in the second part of the book aims to narrow this gap by focusing on decisions that occur in natural settings.

Why should economists be interested in a deeper understanding of pro-social behaviour anyway? Why not just stick to the self-interest hypothesis, which has had great success in many areas outside of economics (for example, Becker, 1976; Stigler, 1984; Frey, 1999; Lazear, 2000a)? There are at least three reasons why it is important to understand the underlying motivation of individuals to behave pro-socially and to test the competing theories empirically:

1. The predominant opinion in economics that self-interest is the single and most important driving force of human behaviour is proven wrong by empirical investigations. Stigler (1981: 176) was therefore wrong when he said, 'Let me predict the outcome of the systematic and comprehensive testing of behaviour in situations where self-interest and ethical values with wide verbal allegiance are in conflict. Much of the time, most of the time in fact, self-interest theory [...] will win.' The bulk of empirical evidence shows that pro-social behaviour is widespread and that pro-social preferences crucially influence economic and societal outcomes. In neglecting the limits of the self-interest theory, some of the most important and most interesting aspects of human behaviour are left unexplained. With theories of pro-social behaviour, testable hypotheses can be derived to explain in which situations self-interest will win and in which situations people behave more pro-socially.

2. The deviation from the self-interest hypothesis has important implications. To derive policy implications on how to foster pro-social behaviour, it is indispensable to have knowledge about whether people react systematically to government interventions (see Nyborg and Rege, 2003). Governments may dampen pro-social behaviour by contributing to public goods, which might crowd out private contributions; governments may also offer (external) incentives to behave pro-socially, like tax reductions; or they may regulate behaviour. Ultimately, in order to design effective institutions, one has to know the conditions under which people are most likely to behave pro-socially. But politicians' incentives in designing such institutions also have to be taken into account. Politicians may not be interested in designing efficient institutions if it hurts their clientele. The fact that even politicians may behave pro-socially is, however, very much disregarded in the literature on 'public choice'.

3. The research on the economics of pro-social behaviour can provide information about methods to elicit voluntary contributions (Steinberg, 1991a; Andreoni, 1998). The majority of charitable organizations depend on private contributions of time and money. But it has to be conceded that, overall, fundraising agencies are probably already intuitively using the right methods to maximize donations. However, theories about pro-social behaviour help to better understand the functioning of the charitable sector in general.

The survey proceeds as follows: Section 2.2 presents explanations for contributions to public goods which are still based on strict self-interest. These 'sophisticated' self-interest theories, however, can only partly explain pro-social behaviour such as charitable donations and volunteering. Section 2.3 presents the three most important sets of theories on non-selfish or 'other-regarding' behaviour: theories based on pro-social preferences, theories based on the norm of reciprocity and approaches that focus on institutional environments. Section 2.4 presents evidence for the effect of relative prices on pro-social behaviour. Section 2.5 discusses the heterogeneity of individuals with respect to pro-social behaviour and the importance of such differences for an economic analysis of pro-social behaviour. In section 2.6, the relationship between utility and pro-social behaviour is discussed. Section 2.7 draws conclusions for policy and formulates remaining open questions.

2.2 THEORIES BASED ON 'EXTENDED' SELF-INTEREST

To explain contributions of money and time to public goods, various theories have been presented which are based on self-interest or use an extended version of the self-interest hypothesis.[4] The two most prominent branches of theories posit either that: (1) the contribution to a public good simultaneously allows the consumption of a private good (for example, people benefit from selective access to some goods, gain prestige or are able to signal their wealth) or that (2) incomplete information about the number of repetitions or about the rationality of the other individuals makes contribution the dominant strategy.

2.2.1 Selective Incentives

In a seminal paper on collective action, Olson (1965) emphasized that people may contribute to a public good if it is a precondition of receiving a private good. In the political sphere, contributions to an interest group or donations to a political party may be motivated by the expectation of receiving a private good. Automobile lobby groups like the AAA, for example, provide breakdown services, insurances and reductions in hotel prices to their members. Donors of arts organizations may gain access to special events, gala dinners, or choice seats in the opera house they support; they may even have exhibition halls named after them. In addition to the aforementioned fringe benefits, volunteers may receive job experience and a social network. Especially for at-home mothers, volunteering can be seen as an investment in human capital and may be used as a re-entry strategy into full employment (Schram and Dunsing, 1981). People contribute, according to this reasoning, to public goods in order to receive a fringe benefit which they otherwise could not get on the market.

Similarly, contributions to public goods, for example donations to a charitable organization, can increase the social standing of a donor (Harbaugh, 1998a) or the donations can signal one's own wealth (Glazer and Konrad, 1996). Especially if geographical distance does not allow signalling one's financial success with other positional goods like yachts or cars, publicized charitable contributions may serve such a purpose. Despite the fact that prestige is not a material good, the important aspect of the 'prestige motive' is that people instrumentally behave pro-socially to get an external reward.

Based on these arguments, the following predictions for individual behaviour can be derived:

SELECTIVE INCENTIVE HYPOTHESIS: If the provision of a private good is responsible for contributions to a public good, i) people will only contribute if selective incentives are offered and ii) they will contribute the minimum amount required to receive the private good.

Some empirical studies have explicitly tested whether fringe benefits are an important motive for pro-social behaviour. Olson (1965) presents circumstantial evidence that the provision of non-collective goods plays a substantial role in labour unions and farmer associations. A more detailed analysis is provided by Buraschi and Cornelli (2002), who try to isolate the effect of the provision of fringe benefits using a donor database of the English National Opera, which keeps track of their donors' donations *and* their consumption of performances and their attendance at special events. The authors find that those people who pay the minimum amount for membership tend to go to special events organized by the opera like dress rehearsals. The authors therefore conclude that access to fringe benefits is an important motivation for becoming a donor. The study, however, has severe shortcomings. Large donations, in particular, cannot be explained by the fringe benefit argument. Furthermore, causality is unclear because only donors can attend special events. It is therefore not surprising that attendance at special events explains 'being a donor'.

The hypothesis that donations may be driven by a desire to signal wealth in order to increase one's prestige is partly supported in studies by Glazer and Konrad (1996) and Harbaugh (1998b). The authors analyse alumni giving to US universities. They have found that people choose to donate an amount just slightly greater than that needed to appear in a certain donations' bracket, as publicized in the alumni journal (for example, a donation of $500–1000). This evidence could support the notion that alumni donate strategically in order to appear in the next higher donations' group. An alternative explanation, however, would stress that the donation brackets may just constitute focal points and therefore donations are grouped just above the lower boundaries of the brackets. Further studies could usefully investigate this issue, including how much the prestige motive is based on social comparison. Probably, the prestige motive has much to do with the donation amount relative to other people.

The aforementioned evidence supports the hypothesis that fringe benefits and prestige are one motivation for pro-social behaviour. Many charities use fundraising techniques which take this motive into account. For instance, they organize dinners where social comparison between potential donors is used as a method to increase donations. However, the theory can only partly explain pro-social behaviour. Empirically, the provision of selective incentives can only explain 'voluntary' contributions of money and time to public goods in isolated instances. In many situations, however, people donate money without the expectation of receiving a private good. Numerous decisions to contribute are taken anonymously and therefore the provision of fringe benefits is excluded a priori. For example, if nobody knows about a person's pro-social behaviour, recognition in the form of increased prestige cannot be gained externally. In such situations, there is no possibility of receiving a private good or recognition from others as an external (material) reward for pro-social behaviour.

2.2.2   Incomplete Information

According to standard game theory, it is rational for self-interested subjects to cooperate in infinitely repeated public goods games. To cope with the fact that people also cooperate to a certain extent in finitely repeated public goods games, game theorists were obliged to rethink their models. The introduction of two kinds of incomplete information into repeated games changes the prediction that people do not cooperate in such situations. Firstly, if the end point of a repeated interaction is stochastically determined, subjects with low discount rates may reach optimal or near optimal outcomes (Fudenberg and Maskin, 1986). Secondly, if individuals are uncertain whether one subject 'irrationally' reciprocates cooperation with cooperation, purely selfish actors may choose to cooperate in early stages and defect in later rounds (Kreps et al., 1982). These theories, however, are unable to explain cooperation in on-shot social interactions and cooperation in last rounds.[5]

The theories based on 'extended' self-interest cannot explain the full range of pro-social behaviour. Even in anonymous situations where no material fringe benefit can be expected, people often behave pro-socially. Although some economists are reluctant to accept that the self-interest hypothesis has its limits, the bulk of empirical evidence on pro-social behaviour requires that theories explaining human behaviour go beyond self-interest.

2.3   THEORIES BEYOND SELF-INTEREST

Adam Smith, who praised the selfishness of individuals in *The Wealth of Nations*, did not believe that only selfish motives matter for human beings. In his first book on *The Theory of Moral Sentiments*, Smith wrote that 'How selfish soever man may be supposed, there are evidently some principles in his nature, which interest him in the fortune of others, and render their happiness necessary to him, though he derives nothing from it, except the pleasure of seeing it' (Smith, 1759 [2000]: 3). In recent years, various models have been developed in order to map out *how* man is interested in the fortune of others and whether these motives can systematically explain pro-social behaviour. Three groups of prominent models can be broadly distinguished: (1) theories based on *pro-social preferences* assume that an individual's utility depends directly on the utility of other people; (2) theories of *reciprocity* are based on the notion that individuals behave in a friendly manner when they are treated benevolently and, conversely, they act meanly when treated badly; and (3) a third group of approaches stresses the importance of the *institutional environment* for pro-social behaviour.

The first two theoretical approaches focus more narrowly on motivational factors for pro-social behaviour. For example, researchers consider whether people share some of their possessions because they are motivated by altruism. The third approach focuses more on the institutional environment, which on the one hand influences the importance of the two former motivations, but on the other hand also points to motivations which go beyond pro-social preferences and reciprocity. The definition of property rights, for example, is important. People's willingness to share their possessions decreases substantially if they have earned the money they share, compared to a setting where they find the money on the street or where they get it as a gift.

Importantly, all motives for pro-social behaviour presented in the following sections depend on something other than external reward. People behave pro-socially because they get an internal reward. Individuals have an 'intrinsic motivation' (Deci, 1975; Frey, 1997a) to undertake a certain task, for example to volunteer, to pay taxes, to vote, or to donate money to a good cause.

Each theory predicts different behavioural patterns of individuals. The most pronounced behavioural hypothesis can be made about how people react to the behaviour of others. A special focus of this survey will therefore be placed on how a person motivated either by altruism or by reciprocity reacts to the behaviour of other (public or private) actors. The hypotheses derived from such an approach are then balanced against the existing empirical evidence. In the second part of the book my own empirical results are presented to shed light on pro-social motivations.

2.3.1   Pro-social Preferences

Theories of pro-social preferences are based on the notion that people's utility functions are interdependent. Individuals care not only about their self-interest but also take the well being of others into account. In the three most prominent formulations of pro-social preferences, the utility of others can either (1) influence one's utility directly (pure altruism theories), (2) influence one's utility partly because helping others produces a 'warm glow' (impure altruism theories) or (3) have an effect on one's utility that depends on the difference between one's own and another's well-being (theories of inequality aversion).

2.3.1.1   Pure altruism

Altruism theories assume that others' consumption or utility positively affects an individual's own utility (for example, Becker, 1974; Collard, 1978). People contribute to a public good because they enjoy the well-being of others. Altruistic preferences are used to explain a wide range of pro-social behaviour: donations (Smith et al., 1995), volunteering (Unger, 1991), behaviour in the workplace (Rotemberg, 1994), and contributions in laboratory experiments like dictator games (Eckel and Grossman, 1996a; Andreoni and Miller, 2002). Pure altruists do not care about the source of others' well-being. If, for example, the utility of a welfare recipient increases, the altruist's utility will increase as well, independent of who actually improved the situation of the welfare recipient.

Altruism theories assume that individuals enjoy seeing the well-being of others increase independently of the source of the improvement. This leads to the most important prediction offered by altruism models about the reaction of altruistic individuals to the contribution of others (see, for example, Roberts, 1984):

ALTRUISM HYPOTHESIS: People will contribute positive amounts to public goods but their contributions are inversely related to the contributions of others. If other private individuals or the state contribute to the public good, people will reduce their contribution to the same extent.

The prediction of altruism theories that contributions by others will crowd out an individual's own contribution completely has been criticized on the basis of both theoretical considerations and empirical facts. From a theoretical point of view, for example, it can be argued that in large groups, no altruist would contribute to a public good due to the fact that he or she would free-ride on the contributions of others (Sugden, 1982, Andreoni, 1988). But in reality, people donate to large charities like the Red Cross or Amnesty International. In empirical research, it is difficult to support the one-to-one crowding-out of private contributions by public grants. Government spending has been found to crowd out private contributions, but the crowding-out is far from complete (dollar-for-dollar); it lies in the range of zero to one-half. Ribar and Wilhelm (2002), for instance, find in their analysis of donations to relief organizations that the crowding-out ratio is very small.[6] A \$1 increase of governmental grants reduces private contributions by at most only 23 cents. Similar results can be found for contributions to other public goods like radio broadcasters (Kingma, 1989).[7] In the laboratory, the crowding-out effect can be quite sizeable (for example,

Andreoni, 1993; Bolton and Katok, 1998). The differences between field and laboratory evidence can be either due to differences in group size (Ribar and Wilhelm, 2002) or to the fact that government spending in the field might increase 'moral suasion' by signalling a greater social concern for a public good. In the laboratory, such complementary effects of others' contributions have been found to be absent (Bolton and Katok, 1998). There is, however, an alternative explanation for the results mentioned. Government grants may not only crowd out private contributions due to donors' altruistic preferences, but they may also lower the incentive of charities to undertake fundraising activities. If managers of charities see fundraising as a burden, the flow of government grants may reduce their effort to raise donations.[8] Andreoni and Payne (2003) have empirically established that, for arts organizations and social service organizations, part of the crowding-out indeed comes from the reduction of charities' fundraising efforts when they receive government grants. If fundraising efforts are not included in the estimations, even a low crowding-out effect is likely to be overestimated.

2.3.1.2   Impure altruism

Because pure altruism theories do not make empirically accurate predictions with respect to crowding-out effects, Andreoni (1989, 1990) extends the altruism model with a 'warm glow' motive for giving. People care not only about the utility of the recipient but receive some private goods benefit from their pro-social behaviour *per se*. In comparison with the private goods' benefit mentioned in Section 2.2 (for example, prestige), the 'warm glow' is purely internal, derived from the donor's own knowledge of his pro-social behaviour. Psychologically, various underlying motivations may cause the ultimately egoistic 'warm glow', such as self-reward, negative state relief or guilt reduction (for a survey, see Bierhoff, 2002). In the case of volunteering, self-determination and increased self-esteem may be intrinsically rewarding motives. In models of impure altruism, crowding-out is never perfect because donors still receive a benefit from the donation *per se*. The prediction of the impure altruism model better fits the observation that givers do not see grants as perfect substitutes for private contributions.[9] Nevertheless, the model of 'warm glow' giving still predicts that people will partly reduce their own contributions when other agents or the government increases their share to the public good.

Theories of altruism assume stable interdependent preferences. According to these theories, people will therefore exhibit stable behaviour in favour of others. However, this prediction is at odds with at least two empirical observations. Firstly, pro-social behaviour erodes with repetition in most experimental studies (for example, Dawes and Thaler, 1988). Although in field studies this erosion may be less pronounced, as we will see in the empirical part of the book, altruism theories are not able to explain the decay of pro-social behaviour. Secondly, people do not always behave pro-socially to increase the well-being of others. Sometimes they consciously reduce others' utility by punishing their behaviour, which is inconsistent with altruistic preferences (Fehr and Gächter, 2000a). To cope with these behavioural irregularities, models of inequality aversion focus on the relative well-being of subjects.

2.3.1.3   Inequality aversion

Models of *inequality aversion* assume that one's relative standing in the income distribution is important. According to the model of Fehr and Schmidt (1999), people do not like inequality.[10] Inequality is particularly disturbing when a subject's payoff is smaller than that of other subjects. Such models attempt to explain why, on the one hand, people behave altruistically towards others worse off than they are while on the other hand they punish those who are better off than they are.[11] A number of studies in experimental economics have investigated this phenomenon and found that people's behaviour in various situations can indeed be explained by inequality aversion (Fehr and Schmidt, 1999). However, people are also driven by other motives than inequality aversion. Charness and Rabin (2002), for example, let subjects in a number of simple games choose between an equal payoff (for example, 400,400) and an unequal but often more efficient payoff (750 for the recipient and 400 for the dictator). The authors find 'a strong degree of respect for social efficiency, tempered by concern for those well off' (p. 849), that is the more unequal but socially efficient outcome is often chosen. Whether people are more concerned with social welfare than with inequality has to be investigated further, possibly using a broader set of games than simple dictator games.

   The following theories extend these models by assuming that people care about the well-being of others conditionally on their behaviour and *intentions*.

2.3.2   Reciprocity and Social Comparison

The aforementioned theories of pro-social preferences assume that people value only the distributional consequences of their own and others' behaviour. In theories of reciprocity, people are also concerned about the intentions that lead other people to behavioural choices. We talk of reciprocity when individuals act in a more cooperative manner in response to the friendly behaviour of others and in a hostile way in response to unfriendly behaviour (Sugden, 1984; Rabin, 1993; Falk and Fischbacher, 2001). The reciprocity model has recently gained much attention. It has been claimed that '[p]ractically all life in society includes and implies reciprocities, and reciprocity has been seen as the basic glue that makes people constitute groups or societies' (Kolm, 2000: 115). A substantial number of studies in experimental economics (for example, Fehr and Gächter, 2000b) supplement the evidence provided by other social sciences indicating that reciprocity is an important factor in pro-social behaviour (for sociology, see Gouldner, 1960; and for anthropology, see Sahlins, 1970). In public good games, the option for reciprocally punishing free-riders sustains high contribution rates even with repetition (Fehr and Gächter, 2000a). This is not trivial, as contributions in public good games normally converge to full free-riding over time (Dawes and Thaler, 1988; Ledyard, 1995). Individuals do indeed undertake the costly punishment of free-riders. The more a subject's contribution is below the average of group contributions, the more heavily he or she is punished (Fehr and Gächter, 2000a).

There is also evidence for reciprocity and its influence on pro-social behaviour outside the laboratory. Fong (2001) interprets survey data about support for redistribution as evidence for the importance of reciprocity. People who believe that the needy are necessarily those who have been beset by unfortunate external circumstances are more in favour of redistribution. In contrast, people who believe that the poor are not doing their share to escape poverty are more likely to be against redistribution (see also Bowles et al., 2004). This reflects the view that if the poor do not give or try to give their share to society, they should not receive aid. However, it is also possible that people who are selfish in general will legitimize their behaviour by assuming that welfare recipients are able but unwilling to help themselves. In a second study, Fong (2003) addresses this caveat by randomly matching welfare recipients who report different work morals to potential donors. The results show that people who indicate in a pre-experiment survey that helping the poor is important are especially sensitive to the laziness of welfare recipients. On the one hand, they give large amounts to people who have a high work ethic, while on the other hand they reduce their share substantially when confronted with a lazy person. People who do not indicate in the pre-experiment survey that helping the poor is important are significantly less sensitive to a recipient's laziness.

The principle of reciprocity seems to be important in various fields, from merchandising to political 'logrolling' (a number of examples can be found in Cialdini, 1993), tax compliance (Smith, 1992), tipping in restaurants (Seligman et al., 1985; Conlin et al., 2003) and effort in the workplace (for example, Akerlof, 1982; Frey, 1993; Fehr et al., 1997). To test the effects of reciprocal norms in charitable giving, Falk (2003) conducted a large-scale field experiment where potential donors were provided with either no gift, a small gift or a large gift in the solicitation letter. The relative frequency of donations increases by 75 per cent among those receiving a large gift, compared to the 'no-gift' treatment. If a person receives a gift from a potential aid recipient, the norm of reciprocity seems to require returning a donation. For interactions between donors and recipients, the principle of reciprocity thus seems to play a substantial role. Other studies, however, question the importance of reciprocity for particular forms of pro-social behaviour. Bohnet and Frey (1999a) and Johannesson and Persson (2000) could not support the findings of a previous study by Hoffman et al. (1996) that indicated reciprocity leads to positive contributions in a dictator game.[12] Their studies do not allow for any reciprocity in the experimental setting, but still find substantial positive amounts of giving. Undoubtedly, more research is needed to analyse the conditions under which reciprocity is most important. For the norm of reciprocity, it may be a question not only of the relationship between the donor and a single recipient, but also whether reciprocity affects social interactions *between* donors.

One implication of theories of reciprocity is that people react positively to the behaviour of others. When a group of people have to decide whether to contribute to a public good, individuals will judge the behaviour of others as kind or not, and adjust their behaviour accordingly. If individuals observe that others behave pro-socially, they will do so as well. No one likes being the only one who contributes to a good cause, and no one likes being the 'sucker' who is 'being free-ridden' by others. The most distinctive prediction to such a theory is that individual i's probability of contributing to a public good *increases* when the percentage of individuals j ($j = 1, ..., n; j \neq i$) who contribute increases within a given group. The prediction stands in contrast to the prediction made by altruism theories, where a negative relationship between an individual's own behaviour and the contributions of others in his or her group is expected.

CONDITIONAL COOPERATION HYPOTHESIS: People's pro-social behaviour is conditional on the behaviour of others. The individual behaviour varies positively with the average behaviour in the group.

The idea of *conditionality* in theories of reciprocity is crucial. Individuals are defined as conditional cooperators when the positive correlation discussed above applies. This theoretical prediction is based on a broad notion of social comparison. The idea that the more others contribute, the more one gives, may be based on three motivational reasons. Firstly, people have some sort of reciprocal preferences, as mentioned above. Secondly, people may want to behave in an appropriate way and to conform to a social norm. The behaviour of others signals what one 'should' do, and people do not wish to deviate from the social norm (Messick, 1999; Cialdini and Goldstein, 2004). Or thirdly, contributions by others may serve as a signal for the quality of the public good, or of the organization which provides the good in the end (for example a charity, see Vesterlund, 2003; Andreoni, 2005; Romano and Yildirim, 2001). The few studies which try to ascertain in a laboratory setting whether people undertake social comparison out of conformity or reciprocity mostly conclude that their results cannot be explained by reciprocity, but rather by conformity or signalling (Schroeder et al., 1983; Bohnet and Zeckhauser, 2002; Bardsley and Sausgruber, 2002; Potters et al., 2005). However, Falk et al. (2003) let their subjects play two separate public good games simultaneously. The authors find two social interaction effects: firstly, people give more to the group with high cooperation rates and, secondly, the contribution within one group depends positively on others' contributions. The behaviour in this experimental setting cannot be explained by conformity, but indicates that people reciprocally contribute more to the group when cooperation by others is more pronounced.

There are two ways of testing reciprocity and in particular 'conditional cooperation':

1. Expectations about the behaviour of others should positively correlate with one's own behaviour, as found in various studies (see, for example, Dawes et al., 1977; Selten and Ockenfels, 1998; Croson, 1998). For example, there is a large literature showing that people's (self-reported) tax compliance correlates with their estimate of other people's non-compliance (for example, Kaplan and Reckers, 1985; Webley et al., 1988; Bosco and Mittone, 1997). However, this kind of evidence does not reveal the direction of causality. It may be the case that expectations do not trigger behaviour, but rather that behaviour influences expectations. Such a 'false consensus' effect (Dawes et al., 1977; Ross et al., 1977; Marks and Miller, 1987) can occur because one projects one's own behaviour onto others, or because behaviour needs to be justified.

2. In a laboratory experiment, which allows one to vary the average behaviour of the group at random, Fischbacher et al. (2001) solved the causality problem by using the strategy method. Subjects in their laboratory public good game have to decide how much to give to a public account, on the basis of the contributions of others. The study concludes that roughly 50 per cent of the people increase their contribution if the others do so as well.[13] Importantly, Fischbacher et al. argue that conditional cooperation explains the decrease of contributions with repetition, which can be observed in almost all repeated fairness experiments (for example, Dawes and Thaler, 1988). People observe the behaviour of others and give slightly less. Such an incomplete matching of others' contributions will lead to an erosion of pro-social behaviour over time. However, in many real-life situations like participation in

elections and paying taxes, no such erosion is observed, although exact feedback of the participation rate, at least for voting, is available. There are of course a number of situations where public goods are not provided. It seems that much more has to be known about situations in which conditional cooperation will lead to an erosion of pro-social behaviour and vice versa. This point is discussed further in the empirical analysis in Chapter 4.

A number of other public good experiments do not test the effects of social comparison explicitly, but the results show that individual contributions vary with the mean contribution of the group (for example, Offerman et al., 1996; Croson, 1998; Keser and van Winden, 2000; Brandts and Schram, 2001; Kurzban et al., 2001; Albert et al., 2002; Tyran and Feld, 2002; Tyran, 2004; Andreoni and Samuelson, 2005). In contrast to most studies about conditional cooperation, which are based on laboratory experiments, Andreoni and Scholz (1998) provide a non-laboratory study, finding that one's own donation depends on the donations of one's reference group. The results show that, if the contribution of those in one's social reference group increases by an average of 10 per cent, the expected rise in one's own contribution is about 2-3 per cent. However, because the reference group in this study is constructed on socio-economic characteristics, it does not provide a direct test of how people react to the behaviour of others.[14]

In a very interesting field experiment on tax compliance, Wenzel (2001) asked taxpayers in a first step about their own tax compliance and about others' norms and behaviour with regard to paying taxes. In the field experiment, he informed a subgroup of these taxpayers about their misperception of others' behaviour. Taxpayers, actually, wrongly think that most others act less honestly than they themselves do. When people are informed in the experiment that others are more honest than they expected them to be, they subsequently significantly reduced their claims for tax reductions (in their actual behaviour) compared to the control group. This result can be interpreted as evidence that people behave conditionally on what others do.[15] Heldt (2005) presents evidence in support of conditional cooperation in the field. In an innovative study, he found that cross-country skiers are more likely to contribute to the maintenance of the slopes if confronted with many others who do so. Shang and Croson (2005) show in a field experiment that people increase their financial contribution in a National Public Radio campaign when informed about a high contribution of just the previous donor. Another field experiment that can be interpreted as evidence for 'conditional cooperation' is presented by List and Lucking-Reiley (2002). The authors analyse the impact of 'seed money' on charitable donations. 'Seed money' denotes the share of a public good already collected when looking for additional donors. When the authors exogenously increased the 'seed money' (which can be interpreted as the donations by others) from 10 per cent to 67 per cent, donations increased by a factor of six, with an effect on both participation rates and contribution levels. This result may also be interpreted as a positive correlation between the giving of others and the giving of the individual donor. A positive correlation has also been found in a situation where money is collected in a community using a list of others in the neighbourhood who had already donated. The longer the list, the higher the willingness to contribute (see, for example, Reingen, 1982).

In sum, there are a number of studies analysing the influence of a norm for reciprocity on pro-social behaviour. Field studies are, however, very rare. In Chapter 4, an empirical study is presented which tests for conditional cooperation in a naturally occurring decision situation.

2.3.3   Institutional Environment

For pro-social behaviour, the institutional environment in which people decide to contribute time and money to public goods is crucial (for example, Ostrom, 2000; Sobel, 2002: 146-9). The institutional environment can be defined as 'the set of fundamental political, social and legal ground rules that establish the basis for production, exchange and distribution' (Davis and North, 1971: 71). The institutional environment, which constitutes the context in which people decide, can matter even though the decisions remain the same in terms of material payoffs. Such context-dependent pro-social behaviour has been labelled 'institutional framing' by Isaac et al. (1991).

The influence of the institutional environment on pro-social behaviour can be twofold. On the one hand, the context calibrates the salience of motives like altruism and reciprocity. In a situation where a mechanism exists to punish free-riders, the norm of reciprocity will be more important than in the absence of this institutional feature. On the other hand, the institutional environment can trigger motives which go beyond altruism and reciprocity, as evidence presented by Bohnet and Frey (1999a, 1999b) and Frey and Bohnet (1995) suggests. In a dictator game they allow for one-way identification, meaning that the dictator sees the recipient but not vice versa. This institutional change increases the willingness to cooperate dramatically. Such a shift in behaviour can be explained neither by altruism nor by reciprocity, because according to these theories identification should not change the behaviour in the decision situation. Giving in dictator games may therefore not solely be caused by reciprocity (for example, Hoffman et al., 1996) or altruism (for example, Johannesson and Persson, 2000).

The effect of contextual factors on pro-social behaviour is supported in various experiments, where framing the same decision differently has a critical influence on decisions (see, for example, Andreoni, 1992; Sonnemans et al., 1998; Elliott et al., 1998; Cookson, 2000). Even the labelling of the same prisoner's dilemma game as either a 'community game' or a 'Wall Street game' changes behaviour significantly. Whether cooperation in the 'community game' is higher due to a change in the salience of the social norm or in the expectations about other people's reactions, however, is an open question (see Bohnet and Cooter, 2003). Because framing effects are significant, most experimentalists try to avoid using verbal cues in their decision settings. However, verbal framing is not the only contextual factor which influences human pro-social behaviour. Real-life social contexts contain a variety of cues which shape individuals' beliefs about the appropriate set of rules. This is closely related to findings in ultimatum game experiments conducted in 15 cultures: 'the preferences over economic choices [...] are shaped by the economic and social interactions of everyday life' (Henrich et al., 2001: 77). The institutional environment can have at least two distinctive effects:

1. *The institutional environment changes the salience of a social norm*
   Institutional settings as well as framing effects change the focus of what is considered to be fair behaviour in a certain situation. The context helps to evaluate which set of values to use. Whether people share $10 that they have received as a gift or, by contrast, that they have had to earn does indeed influence the 'generosity' of the donor considerably. In dictator games between students, an equal split of the total seems to be the norm for donors. When the same amount of money has to be shared with a charity, the amount given is on average much larger (Eckel and Grossman, 1996a). People behave like 'conditional altruists' (Konow, 2003a) whose pro-social behaviour is dependent on the setting. According to Bohnet and Frey (1999b), the contextual setting influences the social distance and thereby varies the empathy between the actors. Charities have long recognized the importance of reducing social distance between donor and recipient. One often-used technique to trigger empathy is to allow for sponsor-specific recipients. It is well known that people are more willing to help an 'identifiable victim' (Schelling, 1968), like a specific child in the Third World, than to support a project which tries to improve the overall situation of children in poor countries.[16]

   More generally, contextual factors not only change the social distance between the individuals, but also influence the salience of a social norm in contributing to a public good. It can be hypothesized that 'the greater the extent to which a decision is taken in a social context, the more relevant manners become' (Bohnet and Frey, 1999b: 44).

2. *The institutional environment varies the degree of (potential) social sanctions* The context in which people decide to contribute to a public good affects the extent of social sanctions when the social norm is violated. Even in anonymous situations, people may follow the internalized social norm because they otherwise suffer from guilt, shame or fear (Coleman, 1990). According to Trivers (1971), internalized norms are a reaction to social sanctions in case of the violation of a norm. Even the suspicion that someone dislikes one's behaviour can trigger compliance (see Brennan and Pettit, 1993; Loewenstein, 2000). Social sanction, for example in the form of social approval or disapproval, is most important if each person's identity is revealed. In situations where anonymity is lifted, pro-social behaviour is expected to be the most pronounced (Rege and Telle, 2004). Soetevent (2005) examines the role of anonymity in a field experiment in Dutch churches. Either 'closed' collection bags or open collection baskets were randomly used for the collection of offerings. The open baskets, where the neighbours on each side can identify the donor's contribution, increase contribution in the services' second offering by 10 per cent. Interestingly, people started to give larger coins when open baskets were used.

To illustrate the importance of the institutional environment, three different phenomena will be discussed which substantially influence pro-social behaviour: (1) property rights; (2) in-group effects; and (3) communication.

1. *Property rights* The perception of what constitutes a fair allocation is shaped greatly by the way property rights are assigned (see Frey and Bohnet, 1995; Gächter and Riedl, 2003). Imagine the following situation with two different environments: you submit an academic paper for a prize, as does your colleague. In one setting, the independent jury chooses your paper to receive a $1000 prize. In the other setting, the independent jury could not choose between your paper and your friend's paper, but a lottery was used to determine that you will receive the cash prize. Would you share the money prize with your friend? Probably only in the situation where you received the property rights by luck. The way of assigning the property right changes the principles of what is perceived as a fair share. Cherry et al. (2002) investigated whether in a laboratory dictator game the allocation differed when earned wealth was divided compared to unearned wealth given by the experimenter. In the treatment where people received the money as a gift, only 15 per cent offered nothing to the recipients. In sharp contrast, when people had to

earn the $40 which was to be divided by answering some questions, 70 per cent of the subjects offered nothing to the other person. It seems that less generosity can be expected when people attribute the received property rights to a variable that they can influence (for example, effort). In contrast, when the assignment of a property is based on factors that cannot be influenced (luck), an equal sharing is perceived to be fairer (Konow, 2000; Hoffman and Spitzer, 1985). One should expect that the stronger the property rights that are assigned, the less likely individuals will be to share their wealth equally.

2. *In-group effects*   The institutional environment may shape the formation and salience of groups. For example, whether individuals are faced with a decision to behave pro-socially in their own firm or in the supermarket is critical for their decision (Carpenter et al., 2005). There is overwhelming evidence suggesting that people tend to cooperate more with their in-group (for example, other members of the same fraternity) than with individuals not part of their in-group (like members of other fraternities) (see, Kollock, 1998). Even a minimal definition of groups (for example, those who prefer Kandinsky over Klee) has been found sufficient to create a group identification that has a significant influence on the division of money in an experimental setting (Tajfel, 1981). In-group effects can also been found outside the laboratory. The more equal and less fragmented a community is in terms of ethnicity and race, the greater is the willingness to participate in social organizations and activities (for example, Alesina and La Ferrara, 2000), and the greater is the acceptance of income redistribution (for example, Luttmer, 2001). One reason for the higher contribution rates in in-groups may be that in a defined group, individuals have a biased perception about members of their own group and those of the out-group. In the case of redistribution, people may attribute the poverty of a group member to external circumstances (such as bad luck), whereas a poor outcome for a non-group member tends to be attributed to poor personal characteristics.[17] The tendency to help in-group members may also be due to various other reasons, like reciprocity, social pressure or sociobiological motives.

3. *Communication*   A number of studies have empirically shown that communication is important for cooperation in social dilemmas (for a meta-analysis, see Sally, 1995), despite the fact that no enforceable agreements can be made and communication is therefore viewed as 'cheap talk' (Farrel and Rabin, 1996). Communication fulfils two important functions.[18] Firstly, people get to know the other people involved; after just a few minutes of talking, the subjects' expectation of others' cooperative behaviour increases significantly in accuracy (Frank et al., 1993b). If people believe that the other group members will not

free-ride, their willingness to contribute increases (according to the hypothesis about 'conditional cooperation' discussed in the last section). Communication, however, has to be face-to-face to affect the judgement of others; when communication is only allowed via a computer, the effects on cooperation are smaller (Ostrom, 2000). Secondly, communication obviously provides an opportunity for subjects to ask other individuals whether they want to contribute to a public good. Most subjects in experiments where communication is allowed try to make agreements about mutual behaviour (Frey and Bohnet, 1995). Even though such agreements can never be enforced, people seldom violate them. People seem to feel obliged to stick to their promises, because the inconsistency of breaking a promise has high psychic costs.[19] 'The Importance of Being Asked' can be demonstrated for the decision to volunteer (Freeman, 1997), to donate money (Long, 1976), to participate in political demonstrations (Opp, 2001) and even for the rescue of Jews in World War II (Varese and Yaish, 2000). The importance of being asked is not only due to selection (people who look like potential volunteers are asked). The requests carry some 'social pressure' with it, and therefore people are more likely to be persuaded by a personal request than by written requests; the probability of contributions is higher the closer the relationship to the requester (Freeman, 1997).

The institutional environment affects pro-social behaviour in various respects. There is, however, still insufficient understanding of 'how a large array of contextual variables affects the processes of teaching and evoking social norms; of informing participants about the behaviour of others and their adherence to social norms; and of rewarding those who use social norms, such as reciprocity, trust, and fairness' (Ostrom, 2000: 154).

2.3.4   Discriminating Between Theories of Pro-social Behaviour

A number of exclusively experimental studies attempt to discriminate between the various theories of pro-social behaviour (see Fehr and Schmidt, 2003). The results are mixed with regard to which model best explains such behaviour. While, for example, reciprocity models are shown to explain behaviour in various public good situations, in other situations, for example dictator games, pro-social behaviour cannot be due to reciprocity. Similarly, some experiments show that people are motivated by inequality aversion, while others support the notion that people are concerned with overall efficiency independent of equality. It is too early to conclude whether one theory is most appropriate to explain pro-social behaviour. In the second part of the book, therefore, further evidence on pro-social behaviour in a naturally occurring setting is presented, which should shed further light on what motivates people to behave pro-socially. Still too little field evidence exists to be able to discriminate between the various theories. An exception is the empirical evidence that government grants do not completely crowd out private contributions to public goods, which supports the notion that people cannot be solely motivated by pure altruism.

The divergent results may show that there is no single motive that can explain pro-social behaviour in general. More likely, the aforementioned motivations are conditional on specific situations. The empirical evidence mentioned in this section points out some conditions which trigger certain motives.

The contributions to a local public good, as simulated in public good experiments, depend on 'conditional cooperation'. If people are confident that they are not being 'free-ridden' by others, they will be prepared to contribute to the public good. However, if people perceive the behaviour of others as consciously free-riding, their willingness to contribute will decrease substantially. People may base their expectations on indicators such as 'seed' money, lists of other contributors or observation of behaviour in past similar decision situations. Such 'conditional cooperation' can be interpreted as reciprocity or conformity. Because some people are prepared to bear costs to punish 'selfish' behaviour, the possible enforcement of norms will also urge 'selfish' individuals to behave pro-socially. This reciprocity motive can be detected especially in the self-governance of common-pool resources (Ostrom, 1990) and in laboratory public good experiments (Fehr and Gächter, 1998). Of course, other factors matter as well, such as the degree of anonymity, whether communication is possible, whether the decision is repeated, how large the marginal returns on contributions are, and what the size of the group is. The salience of interdependent utility in small groups is likely to be an important reason why reciprocity is crucial in this context. Everybody knows that the free-riding of a minority decreases the individual's payoff. However, in situations where interdependence is not as salient, 'conditional cooperation' may not be as important. For example, whether your neighbour contributes to the World Wildlife Funds or not does not obviously influence your well-being. It is therefore important to better understand which conditions trigger the various motives, such as whether conditional cooperation is sensitive to group size, and whether people care only for their reference group. It is conceivable that people do not care how many individuals contribute to public radio in total, but that they do care whether their reference group does.

In the case of charitable giving or 'dictator game' situations, reciprocity is less important and sometimes even not possible due to the decision situation. It is hard to imagine that a street child in Brazil will ever reciprocate a donation. Altruism and 'warm glow' giving can, however, explain the large amount of money donated. The probability of pro-social behaviour increases with the degree of identification (Bohnet and Frey, 1999b) and with the neediness of the recipient. Altruism and 'warm glow' giving is very sensitive to contextual factors, because with a slight variation in the institutional environment, the expected 'warm glow' can change. The same can be said about the more general phenomenon of intrinsic motivation. As more fully discussed in the following section, the design of institutions can dramatically influence the intrinsic motivation to behave pro-socially. Whether people think that their contribution behaviour is voluntary or whether they perceive it to be enforced is an important factor in the pleasure they get from pro-social behaviour and ultimately influences the extent of such behaviour.

In sum, there is still a lot to learn about the motives for pro-social behaviour. The focus has to be more on which conditions may trigger the various motives for pro-social behaviour. As is undertaken in the second part of this book, more field evidence needs to complement the findings from laboratory experiments. In the following sections, two other important factors for the understanding of pro-social behaviour are discussed: the importance of monetary incentives and heterogeneity with respect to pro-social behaviour.

2.4 MONETARY INCENTIVES AND PRO-SOCIAL BEHAVIOUR

From an economic point of view, people's pro-social behaviour should depend on the relative cost of behaving that way: the more 'expensive' pro-social behaviour is, the less it should be undertaken. Relative prices and incentives can be understood as important factors in the institutional environment discussed above. In this section, the effects of monetary incentives on pro-social behaviour are investigated in more detail. According to standard economic theory, if contributing time and money to public goods becomes less expensive, people should undertake these activities more.

When people react systematically to changes in the cost of pro-social behaviour, this opens up the opportunity to subsidize pro-social behaviour in order to increase it. In the case of charitable giving, there are two possible approaches to subsidizing pro-social behaviour. Firstly, donors can receive a rebate on the donated amount. In various countries, people are able to deduct their charitable giving from their taxable income. When a person faces a marginal tax rate of 20 per cent, a donation of \$1 only costs \$0.8, because this person will save \$0.2 in taxes. The price of a donation with tax deductions is therefore $1 - s$ where s represents the tax rate. Secondly, a third party can match donations. Besides the public sector, this mechanism is popular in a number of corporations in the USA and Europe, where employers match charitable contributions made by their employees. To contribute a total of $1, the donor has only to donate $0.8 which will be matched by $0.2. A matching rate is equivalent to a rebate rate when $s_m = s/(1 - s)$. Such monetary incentives to increase pro-social behaviour can of course be implemented in all areas where pro-social behaviour is involved: volunteering, littering, organizational citizenship behaviour, and so on. In what follows, two contradictory effects of monetary incentives on pro-social behaviour are presented: (1) according to the ordinary *relative price effect*, pro-social behaviour will increase when monetary incentives are provided; (2) in certain circumstances, monetary incentives may, however, decrease intrinsic motivation to undertake the pro-social behaviour due to a *motivational crowding-out effect* (Frey, 1997a). The net effect of monetary incentives on pro-social behaviour may be positive or negative in such circumstances, depending on the magnitude of the two effects. Under specific conditions, the relative price effect can thus be reversed.

2.4.1   Relative Prices of Pro-social Behaviour

The importance of the relative price effect for pro-social behaviour can be illustrated by the opposition of very wealthy US citizens to a recent tax reform proposal. A group of rich citizens centred around Bill Gates, the founder of Microsoft, has been arguing against the introduction of a new tax law that would basically lower the tax burden for wealthy people. This unusual opposition against tax reductions, especially the repeal of the bequest tax, asserts that charitable giving would be reduced dramatically as a result of the tax cuts: 'Philanthropy is not solely inspired by the tax code, but the estate tax unquestionably provides a powerful incentive for charitably oriented people to stretch their giving. Estate tax repeal will most likely reduce charitable giving and bequests' (Gates and Collins, 2002).

A substantive literature attempts to analyse whether the presumption that people react to the price of giving is founded on a solid empirical basis (for a survey, see Andreoni, 2004). Three results of this branch of research are worth mentioning.

Firstly, estimated price elasticities support the hypothesis that the price of giving is important for pro-social behaviour. Due to a number of empirical problems, the estimated elasticities vary from -0.4 to -3.0, but most fall in a range from -1.0 to -1.3 (Andreoni et al., 1996). Recent studies based on panel data find somewhat lower price elasticities in the range from -0.51 to -1.26 (for example, Randolph, 1995; Auten et al., 2002). This means, for example, that the elimination of tax deductibility for charitable contributions would increase the price of a unit of giving for a taxpayer formerly faced with a marginal tax rate of 30 per cent from 0.7 to 1.0. Calculating the effect equivalently, charitable contributions would decrease between 15 per cent and 36 per cent. In laboratory experiments, for example dictator games, a falling demand curve has also been observed (Andreoni and Miller, 2002).[20]

Secondly, substitutes and complements have to be taken into account when analysing the relative price effect on pro-social behaviour. Charitable contributions, for example, can be made in cash (charitable giving) or time (volunteering). If monetary giving and volunteer labour are complements, the aforementioned tax deduction would also increase volunteering. If, however, people move away from volunteering when prices for cash contributions decrease, the benefits of such a decrease would be overestimated by ignoring the effect on volunteering. Contrary to standard economic theory, contributions of time and money are mostly found to be gross complements (Brown and Lankford, 1992; Andreoni et al., 1996; Freeman, 1997).[21] The effect of a price reduction on pro-social behaviour is therefore understated by focusing solely on monetary giving.

Thirdly, the price of charitable contributions, according to economic theory, should also depend on opportunity costs. This is, however, seldom confirmed. Especially for volunteering, the opportunity cost of time (that is, individual wages) can hardly explain differences in volunteer activities (see Freeman, 1997). Unemployed persons offer less volunteer labour, although they have lower opportunity costs for their time, and with rising income, people increase their volunteering instead of substituting it for cash donations.

The spectrum of situations in which monetary incentives matter for increasing pro-social behaviour is much wider than just tax reductions for charitable contributions considered in the studies discussed so far. In many further situations differences in relative prices explain a large degree of the variation in pro-social behaviour. For example, to increase environmental protection, monetary incentives are being considered or are already implemented. An illustrative case is presented by Diekmann (1995). The author compares the consumption of electricity by people in the city of Berne with the corresponding consumption by people in Munich. While in both cities people report the same level of concern for environmental problems and have similar intentions towards ecological responsibility, in Munich 69 per cent of the people reported that they reduced the heating when leaving the house or apartment for a longer time, while in Berne only 23 per cent did so. It comes as no surprise to the economist that the difference can be explained by the fact that in Munich many more households have an individual heating bill than in Berne.

To summarize, the research on price elasticities of charitable contributions and behaviour in various incentive situations supports the view that people react to changes in relative prices. However, many of the observed patterns cannot be explained by relative prices alone, and it is difficult to account for the level of pro-social behaviour. Surprisingly, the introduction of the price mechanism in areas formerly based on purely voluntary contributions can backfire under certain conditions. This is the case when the motivational crowding-out effect dominates the relative price effect. The next section discusses the theoretical foundations of and the empirical evidence for this motivational crowding-out effect.

2.4.2   Motivational Crowding Effect

The law that is probably most important in economics, the relative price effect, does not always hold. In certain situations, a motivational crowding-out effect can work against the relative price effect (Frey, 1997a). This is of considerable importance for pro-social behaviour. Due to the underlying incentive structure, contributions in social dilemmas are not utility-maximizing in strictly monetary terms. People who contribute in an anonymous situation to a public good must have an intrinsic motivation to do so. Incentives may undermine or even crowd-out a motivation to behave pro-socially (Bénabou and Tirole, 2004). Incentives can be understood in a narrow sense as positive or negative monetary incentives (rewards or punishments). In a broader understanding, all sorts of regulations can yield a motivational crowding effect.

The motivational crowding effect was known in psychology long before economists started to think seriously about the 'hidden costs of reward' (Lepper and Greene, 1978) or the 'corruption effect' (Deci, 1975). An exception is Titmuss's book on *The Gift Relationship* (Titmuss, 1970), where he argues that monetary incentives for blood donors will undermine their motivation and reduce the amount of blood donated overall. Whereas Titmuss did not present any serious empirical evidence, a considerable amount of evidence has since been collected on the motivational crowding-out effect (for an extensive survey, see Frey and Jegen, 2001). In psychology, the large number of experimental studies on the crowding effect has led to several meta-analyses that in general support the finding that (external) incentives have detrimental effects on intrinsic motivation (for example, Deci et al., 1999).[22] In economics, the few studies which explicitly test the crowding-out effect cover a wide range of activities involving pro-social behaviour. This section limits discussion to the three cases of volunteering, civic duties and trust relationships.[23]

The introduction of monetary incentives has been found to reduce the *work motivation of volunteers* (Gneezy and Rustichini, 2000; Frey and Götte, 1999). Frey and Götte show in an econometric study that, while the size of the offered financial reward raises the number of hours volunteered, the mere fact that financial compensation is provided significantly reduces the amount of volunteering. Volunteers receiving the median amount of monetary incentive work less than either people who receive a large reward or those who receive *no* reward at all, a result that supports the crowding-out effect and has, of course, important implications for policies regarding volunteer work. The evidence points especially to two important aspects of the crowding effect:

1. The introduction of (external) incentives does not change the compensation scheme marginally from zero monetary incentives to very little compensation, but it dramatically shifts the perception of the decision situation on the whole. In the situation with extrinsic incentives, people seem to behave in an 'exchange mode', where they make strategic considerations and start to calculate ('I am not working for only $5 per hour, am I?') (Gneezy, 2003). In contrast, in a situation without external incentives, people seem rather to behave in a 'moral mode' where pro-social behaviour is rewarded internally, such as with a 'warm glow'.

2. Small amounts of extrinsic incentives in particular are expected to have large negative effects on observed pro-social behaviour, because with large extrinsic incentives the relative price effect will dominate. This is supported in a field experiment by Gneezy and Rustichini (2000), who offered extrinsic incentives to children who voluntarily collected monetary donations. Small extrinsic incentives are found to reduce the motivation of volunteers significantly, while the relative price effect dominates when large incentives are offered. This effect can be observed with negative incentives (fines) as well as with positive incentives (rewards) (Gneezy, 2003).

Other important crowding effects have been discovered for activities which require intrinsic motivation in the form of *civic duty*. Frey and Oberholzer-Gee (1997) investigate motivational crowding-out in the context of siting locally undesirable projects (so-called 'Not In My Backyard' or NIMBY problems). Economic theory proposes a simple solution for such projects, which are often socially desirable but impose considerable costs on the immediate neighbours; communities which host the NIMBY project should be compensated by all the other communities, so that their net benefit becomes positive. Frey and Oberholzer-Gee analysed the reaction of Swiss residents to such compensation for the acceptance of a nuclear waste depository. While more than 50 per cent of the respondents agreed to host the depository without compensation, the offering of monetary incentives reduced the acceptance rate to 24 per cent. The authors' favoured explanation for this reduction is that the sense of civic virtue that accompanies accepting the noxious facility is crowded out by the offer of monetary compensation. Civic duty to behave pro-socially can be crowded out not only by explicit monetary incentives, but also by the design of a constitution. An important application of this notion is tax morale, where the crowding effect can have huge costs. Tax morale, or the motivation that explains the 'low' tax evasion in many countries, depends to a great extent on trust between the government and the citizens. A constitution which tries to discipline citizens can be perceived as distrusting and therefore decrease civic virtue (see Frey, 1997b for empirical evidence).

More generally, the introduction of monetary incentives can have considerable negative effects on *trust*-based pro-social behaviour. In a laboratory experiment with CEO's, Fehr and List (2004) found that detrimental effects follow from external incentives. If the first player uses an external incentive in a trust game, the second player returns less money. However, the highest efficiency is reached if it is possible to implement an external incentive but certain subjects explicitly trust in each other, so that they do not use the incentive mechanism. Therefore, while in general trust is crowded out by external incentives, incentives also seem to allow for exhibiting trust when they are explicitly not used.[24] The authors interpret the negative effect of incentives in terms of reciprocity. The explicit threat to punish shirking is perceived as distrust and a reciprocal agent increases shirking as a response to such a hostile act. Bohnet et al. (2001) conducted a study where subjects have to decide whether they want to enter a contract without knowing whether the partner will perform. Economic theory expects that a higher probability of contract enforcement will increase contract performance. The authors, however, report a crowding-out effect: in a situation of weak contract enforcement, trustworthiness (that is, people do perform contracts) is higher than in a situation of medium contract enforcement; only if contract enforcement is increased well past the medium mark are contracts performed again. The findings support the notion that medium or low incentives can crowd out trust and intrinsic motivation.

Without doubt, it cannot be expected that extrinsic incentives *always* lead to a motivational crowding effect. The present state of research allows one to indicate conditions under which extrinsic incentives have more positive or more negative effects. A discussion of these identifiable conditions makes it clear that crowding effects are of particular importance for pro-social behaviour:

1. Intrinsic motivation can only be crowded out by extrinsic incentives if people have an intrinsic motivation to begin with. If, for example, people only undertake a task due to extrinsic motivation, an increase in extrinsic incentives will certainly increase effort, as predicted by standard price theory. However, to contribute time or money to a public good often involves some sort of intrinsic motivation. The introduction of external incentives to increase pro-social behaviour must therefore be considered very carefully.

2. A motivational crowding-out is expected if the external intervention is perceived as *controlling*. Psychologically, extrinsic incentives can have negative effects when they reduce the perceived self-determination of individuals (Rotter, 1966; Deci, 1975), or when they interfere with a relationship based on mutual trust (Rousseau, 1995). As self-determination and trust are important for pro-social behaviour, the introduction of external incentives can seriously reduce the intrinsic joy of behaving pro-socially. However, if extrinsic incentives are applied carefully, for example acknowledging individuals' intrinsic motivation, they may not be perceived as hostile and controlling, and can even support and increase pro-social behaviour (the crowding-in effect).

3. A motivational crowding-out effect only results in a net negative effect on behaviour if it dominates the standard relative price effect. As mentioned before, this is most likely to be the case for (positive or negative) incentives that are small. Motivational crowding, however, is not thereby rendered irrelevant in the context of pro-social behaviour. Firstly, there are many situations where small incentives are quite important. In the case of pro-social behaviour, the introduction of small incentives is widely discussed, as in the context of volunteering. Secondly, the reliance on extrinsic incentives may lead to a selection of certain 'selfishly' oriented people. Whereas for some tasks it is desirable to attract extrinsically motivated people (see, for example, Lazear, 2000b), in other areas like the non-profit or charitable sector this is not very welcome (for example, Besley and Ghatak, 2005). Thirdly, if by the crowding effect pro-social preferences are affected permanently, pro-social behaviour will not reach the original level again, even if the extrinsic incentive is removed.[25] Fourthly, extrinsic incentives for a certain task may not only reduce the intrinsic motivation for the particular task, but also spill over to other areas (Frey and Benz, 2000). Even small incentives may then destroy intrinsic motivation in areas that are actually not subject to the external intervention. The detrimental effect of extrinsic incentives may even be worse in the dimension not directly affected.

To summarize, extrinsic incentives can crowd out intrinsically motivated pro-social behaviour if the external intervention is perceived as controlling by the individuals affected. This effect is supported in a large number of laboratory experiments and in some field studies. If the motivational crowding effect is strong and dominates the standard economic relative price effect, an extrinsic incentive can lead to a negative overall effect on behaviour. As intrinsic motivation in one form or another is essential for pro-social behaviour, the motivational crowding effect is of particular importance in this context.

2.5   HETEROGENEITY IN INDIVIDUALS

In standard economic theory, preferences are usually assumed to be homogeneous. This unrealistic assumption is often no obstacle to derive powerful predictions, even with regard to pro-social behaviour. However, taking the variation in pro-social attitudes into account leads to interesting additional implications. To begin with, there are significant differences between individuals: Andreoni and Miller (2002) show in a study based on dictator games that about 47 per cent of individuals' behaviour can be characterized as selfish (however, only 23 per cent are perfectly selfish), while the behaviour of the other 53 per cent has to be characterized as 'other regarding'. Fischbacher et al. (2001) find in a public good game that 30 per cent of the individuals behave like free-riders and 50 per cent can be characterized as 'conditional cooperators'. Psychologists have for decades distinguished individual motivations using survey answers. They typically classify people into four types: altruists, who care only for the utility of others; competitors, who want to do better than their counterparts; cooperators,[26] who pursue the best for themselves and the others; and individualists, who only look out for themselves (Kelley and Stahelski, 1970; McClintock, 1972). A study by Liebrand (1984), for example, suggests that individuals can be classified as 5 per cent altruists, 10 per cent competitors, 31 per cent individualists and 53 per cent cooperators.[27]

But why should economists deviate from the 'golden rule' of assuming preferences to be given and identical? Why is the heterogeneity of preferences important? At least three reasons for the analysis of heterogeneous pro-social preferences are worth mentioning:[28]

1.   The *interaction of different types* of people is crucial to understanding why cooperation is stable and public goods are provided. Consider, for example, the situation in which an egoistic individual is interacting with a reciprocal individual. The presence of a reciprocal individual may

change the material incentive of the egoist and therefore urge the egoist to behave 'pro-socially'. The presence of only a few reciprocal types may have a big impact on the aggregate outcome of markets and organizations (see the survey in Fehr and Fischbacher, 2002). Whether a pro-social individual will urge an egoist to behave pro-socially or, conversely, a few egoists urge pro-social individuals to start free-riding is a question that depends crucially on the institutional setting. In the absence of punishment for free-riding, are pro-social individuals likely to start behaving in a self-interested way?[29] To analyse the institutions which lead to one of the two cascades, one has to understand how heterogeneous individuals interact.

2. The *institutional environment may influence individuals differently*. In analysing the effect of a change in the institutions, it is important to take people's heterogeneous preferences into account. In the case of tax reductions for charitable contributions, for example, evidence shows that only altruistically inclined people are affected by the change in relative prices (Clotfelter, 1980). People who do not donate to charities are not affected by such a change. Chapter 5 presents additional evidence from a controlled field experiment showing that only certain types of people react to a change in relative prices. In addition, people may react quite differently to the introduction of monetary incentives with respect to their motivation to behave pro-socially (Frey, 2002). Pro-socially inclined people may reduce their intrinsically motivated pro-social behaviour when external incentives are introduced, whereas a selfish individual may react quite differently.

3. The *evolution of heterogeneous pro-social preferences* can help one to understand how pro-social preferences can be fostered. Very little is known about this question in economics. One prominent position, however, is that education can influence pro-social behaviour and probably even preferences. Economics and business students in particular are assumed to be better citizens and better future managers if they are taught some ethics instead of self-interest maximization. Economics students are portrayed as being more egotistical than non-economists, partly because the training changes their behaviour (for example, Frank et al., 1993a, 1996). However, as shown in Chapter 6, it is important to check whether people have heterogeneous pro-social preferences and whether, in the case of economics, those who choose the subject already tend towards egoism when they enter. In that case, it is possible that 'economists are born, not made' (Carter and Irons, 1991).

2.6   A NOTE ON UTILITY AND PRO-SOCIAL BEHAVIOUR

2.6.1   Why should Economists Take Utility into Account?

In the history of ideas, pro-social behaviour has always been linked with human welfare. In the Judeo-Christian tradition, helping others is the only way to reach the ultimate goal of happiness. The founding father of what is called 'virtue ethics', one of the major approaches in normative ethics, is the Greek philosopher Aristotle, who posited that true happiness is found in the practice of virtue. A happy person is thus a moral person.[30] In the Enlightenment, the father of modern economics, Adam Smith, also saw pro-social behaviour as *the* path to well-being: 'Concern for our own happiness recommends to us the virtue of prudence: concern for that of other people' (Smith, 1759 [2000]: 385; cited in Konow and Early 2002). Empirical evidence, however, is still lacking to prove that a person who acts pro-socially is happier than a *homo oeconomicus*, who is solely concerned with his or her narrow self-interest. To answer the question of what constitutes 'the good life', which is also the happy life, one has to understand how pro-social behaviour influences utility (happiness).

Until recently, modern economics has had no statement to make about the content of utility. Utility was assumed to be equivalent to preferences, which could only be measured by looking at revealed behaviour. It has been said that modern economics should not concern itself with utility because, on the one hand, precise knowledge about utility is not important and, on the other hand, utility or well-being cannot in any case be measured (Frey and Stutzer, 2002a: 19-47). Economists are therefore reluctant to accept the notion that there may be ways of measuring utility and for a long time the discipline of economics refused to validate any kind of utility measurement.

In recent years, an ever-growing community of economists have been reconsidering the rejection of utility measurement. They have good reasons to rethink the utility concept because measuring utility enables them to analyse the basic assumption of economics (for example, 'Do people always maximize their utility?') and to discriminate between different models ('Are drug addicts really rational?') (Frey and Stutzer, 2003a). In the case of pro-social behaviour, two important aspects of analysis can be enriched by the utility concept and by measuring well-being:

1.   It is now well established that people violate the basic self-interest hypothesis in various important ways. As mentioned before, pro-social behaviour can be explained by motives such as altruism or some sort of inequality aversion. The measurement of utility allows one to better

discriminate between different theories and to answer questions about whether another person's increase in utility positively affects one's own well-being or whether people actually suffer from inequality.

2.   People can voluntarily make decisions which do not lead to higher utility. They may not even know what exactly makes them happy. There may be a number of reasons why individual decisions are not always welfare-enhancing. People's decisions may, for example, be influenced by a 'projection bias' (Loewenstein et al., 2003), where future utilities are systematically mispredicted because preference adaptation is underestimated. Frey and Stutzer (2003b) elaborate this idea further by showing that people's misprediction of future utility depends on the nature of the good/activity. The benefits from intrinsic goods are systematically underestimated compared to the benefits from extrinsic goods. People may, for example, underestimate the utility they get from volunteering (intrinsic activity) compared to earning money on the market (extrinsic good). Such mispredictions of future utility may lead to suboptimal decisions for *individuals'* welfare. Even if 'helping others' were a source of happiness, individuals would not opt for such activities frequently enough to maximize their utility. Some people even incorporate goals which do not lead to happiness but are instead self-defeating (Schooler et al., 2003). Ryan et al. (1996; see also Kasser and Ryan, 2001) attempt to show that some goals are more satisfying than others, in the sense that people who are oriented towards material and other external rewards are less happy than people who have more intrinsic life goals.

2.6.2   How can Utility be Measured?

A growing literature in economics measures utility in terms of survey answers about happiness or life satisfaction (for surveys, see Easterlin, 2002; Frey and Stutzer, 2002a; 2002b). These measures of subjective well-being, which have been used for decades in psychology (see, for example, Diener et al., 1999; Kahneman et al., 1999), are shown to be valid proxies for utility. The responses to questions like 'How satisfied are you with your life, all things considered?' on a scale from 0-'completely dissatisfied' to 10-'completely satisfied' are correlated with other proxies of happiness like how often people smile, how friends and relatives value a person's well-being, how a person's heart rate and blood pressure indicates response to stress, and so on (see Konow and Earley, 2002). The 'Economics of Happiness' has documented the influence of various factors on individuals' welfare. Starting with Easterlin (1974), who found that although income rose dramatically in the USA, levels of happiness stagnated, a number of subsequent papers on happiness have documented the influence of unemployment (Clark and Oswald, 1994; Winkelmann and Winkelmann, 1998), inflation (Di Tella et al., 2001), political institutions (Frey and Stutzer, 2000), the role of social norms (Stutzer and Lalive, 2004) and excise taxes (Gruber and Mullainathan, 2002). As this branch of research shows that the use of subjective well-being can fruitfully be applied to economic questions, this can now be taken a step further to investigate the effect of pro-social behaviour on happiness.

2.6.3   How Does Pro-social Behaviour Affect Happiness?

The various theories on pro-social behaviour lead to different predictions concerning utility gained from such behaviour. In the following, these predictions are presented alongside the scarce empirical evidence gleaned in economics and evidence documented in psychology and sociology. The focus will be on two theoretical branches: (1) theories of altruism and inequality aversion, and (2) theories of 'warm glow'. Special attention is given to issues of causality.

2.6.3.1   Inequality and happiness

According to theories of altruism and inequality aversion, people's well-being increases if they observe that other people's lives are improving or that inequality between two individuals and/or social inequality is decreasing. Importantly, the increase in utility occurs independently of one's own contribution, whereas according to impure altruism one's own contribution is a substantial source of the 'warm glow' coming from pro-social behaviour. A few studies have investigated the overall effect of inequality as well as the effect of other people's material well-being on individual happiness levels. Alesina et al. (2004) find that people are less likely to report being happy when inequality is high. This 'inequality aversion', however, is more pronounced in Europe than in the USA. Interestingly, the effect of inequality on the well-being of the poor versus the wealthy differs on the two continents. Whereas in the USA only the wealthy seem to suffer from the effect of inequality, in Europe only the well-being of the poor is decreased by higher inequality. However, if 'equality' is a luxury good or a normal good, then rich Europeans should suffer more from inequality than poor Europeans, as is the case in the USA. The authors interpret this result, which is inconsistent with pure inequality aversion, as an effect of differences in social mobility between European countries and the USA. Because social mobility in the USA is perceived to be higher, wealthy US citizens interpret high inequality as a risk of falling down the scale in case of an unfortunate life event. According to the authors, poor US citizens believe that they can improve their income situation substantially if they just make more of an effort. In contrast, poor Europeans feel stuck in poverty. People may therefore not only care about inequality outcomes (whether the income distribution is more or less unequal) but also about the process leading to a certain result (whether it is in the individual's power to influence an outcome).[31] However, Schwarze and Härpfer (2005) find evidence consistent with inequality aversion in Germany for all income classes. In their panel survey, people's life satisfaction is inversely related to inequality on the regional level.

Charness and Grosskopf (2001) find no correlation between happiness scores and preferences for equality in dictator games. Subjects who choose more equal payoffs do not report better well-being *after* the decision, nor do subjects who report higher happiness scores *before* the decision choose more equal payoffs. Thus, the experiment does not support the hypothesis that happiness is correlated with inequality. However, overall happiness measures are explicitly designed not to be too sensitive to minor life events. They are therefore not expected to be influenced by the results in a laboratory experiment involving low stakes. Much more research is needed to understand how the utility levels of others influence one's own happiness.

2.6.3.2   Pro-social behaviour and happiness

Theories of impure altruism predict that pro-social behaviour as such increases utility. Happiness can be achieved by making other people happy. In this branch of research, the focus is on the effect of pro-social behaviour *per se* on subjective well-being. Various studies by psychologists and sociologists, which mostly focus on volunteering, find positive correlations between pro-social behaviour and well-being (for a survey, see Wilson and Musick, 1999). Volunteers report higher well-being scores than non-volunteers; they are less depressed, and their mortality rate is lower than average. These effects are found to be especially true for elderly volunteers (see also Wheeler et al., 1998).

People may get a 'warm glow' from volunteering because helping others increases either their perceived self-esteem or their self-efficacy (Wilson and Musick, 1999: 154). Volunteering may also generate a state of 'flow' (Csikszentmihalyi, 1990), which depends on the extent of commitment, the use of skill and the kind of achievement involved in the task (Argyle, 1999: 364-5). Alternatively, the positive effect of pro-social behaviour in the form of volunteering may be due to the effect of social integration. People who feel integrated and enjoy many personal relationships are taken to be happier than people who feel lonely. According to this explanation, volunteering increases people's well-being not because they help others but because they do it in a group and feel integrated. Most studies on the effects of pro-social behaviour on happiness (mostly on volunteering) cannot discriminate between utility arising from the act of helping and utility arising from 'side-effects' such as social involvement. In addition, most empirical work uses cross-sectional data where participants self-assess the impact of volunteer programme. Apart from problems arising from response biases in volunteers who self-assess the benefits of their own programme, the direction of causality is very difficult to assess in such studies. In fact, pro-social behaviour may not make people happier so much as happier people are more willing to behave pro-socially. There is some evidence that happiness affects one's willingness to help others. In a number of experiments, the mood of subjects was first manipulated, for example, by letting them 'find' a coin or by letting them win in a game. Afterwards, the subjects had the opportunity to help in a task or to donate money to a charity. It is found that those with induced good moods were more likely to help others (Isen and Levin, 1972; Harris and Smith, 1975).[32]

Konow and Early (2002) use simple dictator games to disentangle the various effects that influence the relationship between happiness and pro-social behaviour. The authors ask the subjects various questions about their subjective well-being either before or after a decision on dividing an amount of money between another person and the subjects themselves. The results indicate an indirect relationship between pro-social behaviour and happiness: generosity contributes to self-actualization, which in turn increases long-run happiness. Pro-social behaviour may therefore not immediately increase happiness because 'self-actualizing behaviour may be at odds with short-run happiness' (Konow and Earley, 2002: 21). In the long run, however, pro-social behaviour increases happiness.

Meier and Stutzer (2005) report robust empirical results on whether individuals who volunteer are more satisfied with their life than non-volunteers. The empirical evidence on the relationship between volunteering and life satisfaction is based on the German Socio-Economic Panel (GSOEP) for the period between 1985 and 1999. Life satisfaction is measured on a scale from 1 to 10. The study finds in regressions controlling for time-invariant individual fixed effects that volunteering increases life satisfaction by almost one point. This effect is sizable comparing to the effect of other life events. However, this correlation does not establish causality. Volunteering may not increase life satisfaction, but satisfied people are more likely to volunteer. Such causality problems are pervasive in the earlier literature. The issue of causality is directly addressed in this study by taking advantage of a natural experiment: the collapse of East Germany. Volunteering was still widespread in East Germany when the first wave of data of the GSOEP was collected (shortly after the fall of the Berlin Wall but before the German reunion). Due to the shock of the reunion, a large portion of the infrastructure of volunteering (for example, sports clubs associated with firms) collapsed and people randomly lost their opportunities for volunteering. Based on a comparison of the change in subjective well-being of these people and of people from the control group who had no change in their volunteer status, it is possible to analyse whether volunteering is rewarding in terms of higher life satisfaction. The results establish that volunteering partly *causes* higher life satisfaction.

2.7   CONCLUSION AND OPEN QUESTIONS

The evidence is overwhelming that human behaviour is not solely motivated by narrow self-interest. People accept cost when they voluntarily contribute money or time to public goods and, in a second stage, when they enforce social norms. Such pro-social behaviour is widespread and quantitatively important for economic and societal outcomes. To analyse many aspects of human behaviour, it is essential to better understand motivations beyond self-interest and the conditions under which they prevail. Ultimately, when designing institutions, such as the basic rules applied in a society, pro-social behaviour has to be taken into account. If not, the institutions may not reach their intended goals.

In recent years, a number of theories have evolved which attempt to explain pro-social behaviour. The most important approaches presented in this survey can be classified into three groups: (1) those which emphasize the distributional outcome, as do theories of pro-social preferences; (2) those which highlight the importance of the process that leads to a certain outcome (for example, the intentions of the people involved), an aspect stressed by theories of reciprocity and social comparison; and (3) those which focus on the significance of the institutional environment for pro-social behaviour. The predictions derived from these theoretical approaches are tested against empirical evidence gathered in field studies and laboratory experiments. In particular, the predictions about people's reactions to the pro-social behaviour of others differ quite substantially among the theoretical approaches. Whereas altruism theories predict that people will decrease their contributions to a public good if other persons or the state increases their share, theories of 'conditional cooperation' make exactly the opposite prediction with regard to the behaviour of other individuals. So far, however, there is no field evidence clarifying which of the two theories is better able to explain human behaviour.

The theoretical approaches and the respective empirical studies surveyed in this chapter indicate that it is still too early to make conclusive statements about the importance of the various pro-social motivations. The interrelation between theory and empirical evidence, where theoretical hypotheses are empirically tested and, conversely, empirical results inform and influence theoretical reflections, needs to be put under more pressure in order to better understand pro-social behaviour. However, the survey indicates that many interesting insights can be gained from economics research on pro-social behaviour. Some of the open questions will be addressed in the empirical part of the book.

The most important insight developed in this survey is the effect of the institutional environment for explaining pro-social behaviour. On the one hand, the institutional environment affects the salience of particular social norms, as well as the intrinsic motivation to behave pro-socially. On the other hand, it influences the social interaction between (egoistic and/or altruistic) individuals, as in how the violation of a social norm can be punished. It is, for example, frequently observed that people do not like income inequality and that they especially hate to be worse off than others. In certain institutional settings, however, individuals pursue a socially efficient outcome and accept greater inequality, even if their relative standing in the income distribution is low. How exactly these differences in pro-social behaviour are to be explained by differences in institutions, though, remains an area of substantial future research.

Similarly, a great deal of evidence exists that emphasizes the importance of reciprocity for pro-social behaviour. If the institutional setting allows for the sanctioning of free-riding, such as when the group is small and free-riders can be targeted, high levels of contributions can be achieved. In the interaction between heterogeneous individuals, free-riders are punished and forced to behave pro-socially. But even in the absence of such a mechanism, for example in the case of blood donation or voting, people are prepared to behave pro-socially. In these situations, people seem to have an intrinsic motivation to behave pro-socially that is not conditional on the behaviour of others. Intrinsic rewards from behaving pro-socially again depend on the institutional settings and can either support or destroy the motivation. The question about which institutions increase the salience of reciprocity or influence the intrinsic rewards arising from pro-social behaviour still needs to be explored in more detail.

The survey reveals a great number of open questions, which should guide research on pro-social behaviour in the future. In the second part of the book, three important aspects are addressed:

1. *Social comparison and pro-social behaviour*   A small number of studies reveal that people's pro-social behaviour is conditional on what others do. The willingness to behave pro-socially increases with the average pro-social behaviour of the reference group in the laboratory. This result has to be further investigated in the field. The following

empirical part of the book presents an initial attempt to test 'conditional cooperation' in a field experiment. Such interactional effects are important to understand, because they may explain human behaviour in a variety of situations. For example, crime is almost impossible to fight in areas where nobody obeys the law and nobody wants to be the only one who does so. The conditions under which such a 'bad' equilibrium evolves are not well understood. The same holds for the conditions under which such social comparisons are more or less pronounced. In addition, it is still unclear what motivates the positive correlation between one's own and others' behaviour. Is it due to conformity or reciprocity? Or does the behaviour of others just work as a signal?

2. *Influence of institutions on pro-social behaviour*   Institutions may interact with pro-social behaviour in various ways. For economics, it is important to analyse the effects of changes in relative prices and competition on pro-social behaviour. In the empirical part, the effect of a change in the relative prices is investigated. The overall effects of the interaction between institutions and pro-social behaviour may be at odds with standard economic theory. In particular, the institution of the price system may have serious detrimental effects on pro-social behaviour, because people who behave pro-socially are either motivated by some intrinsic reward or are themselves a special selection of people.

3. *More field evidence*   Future research should be much more based on field evidence. Most empirical research on pro-social behaviour has been based on laboratory experiments. Results from laboratory experiments have greatly improved our understanding of behaviour beyond self-interest. However, it is still unclear how these results apply to the world outside the laboratory, because too few studies exist which test the theories on pro-social behaviour in real-life settings. A special feature of this survey has been to focus on the few existing field studies. Of course, the external validity of field studies comes at the cost of internal validity, but the trade-off has to be evaluated depending on the respective research questions. The best of both worlds can be achieved by undertaking controlled experiments in the field. In the empirical part of the book, a naturally occurring decision setting is analysed and controlled field experiments are undertaken.

Some of these open questions are addressed in the second, empirical part. For the empirical analysis a data set on contributions of students to two social funds at the University of Zurich is used. Chapter 3 presents the data set from the University of Zurich in detail and analyses general patterns of pro-social behaviour; Chapter 4 presents a field experiment which tests for the effect of conditional cooperation on pro-social behaviour; Chapter 5 presents another field experiment which investigates the effect of changes in relative prices on the decision to contribute to the two social funds; and Chapter 6 investigates the effect of education on the willingness to donate. Chapter 7 draws conclusions.

NOTES

1. The multiple m is the marginal return for each individual when he or she contributes one unit to the fund.
2. The amount of volunteering is transformed into the equivalent of full time workers. For an even higher estimation for the USA, see Brown (1999: 25).
3. The following countries are included: Austria, Belgium, Finland, France, Germany, Ireland, Netherlands, Sweden, Spain and the UK. The data were collected in the years between 1995 and 1997. See Anheier and Salamon (1999) for details.
4. This survey does not deal with the argument that people contribute to public goods out of confusion because the respective academic discussion relates mostly to laboratory research (for example, Houser and Kurzban, 2002). It seems absurd to talk of confused individuals when looking at pro-social behavior in real-life situations.
5. Ostrom (1998) discusses the introduction of incomplete information into repeated games more fully.
6. Their analysis is especially valuable as it introduces controls for unobserved institution-specific factors, year-to-year changes in need and changes in organization leadership; factors which may potentially have biased the results of previous studies.
7. See also the results in Okten and Weisbrod (2000), Khanna and Sandler (2000), Payne (1998) and Steinberg (1991b).
8. Fundraising and revenues from ancillary goods constitute a 'necessary evil' for many managers of non-profit organizations (see, for example, Segal and Weisbrod, 1998).
9. Another extension of the pure altruism model assumes that donors value making a difference (Duncan, 2004). In contrast to the impure altruist, the 'impact philanthropist' not only cares about the amount of money he donated, but also whether his donation has a significant impact. The model therefore does not predict a dollar-for-dollar crowd-out as predicted by the pure altruism model. Moreover, it suggests that others' contribution do crowd out giving more than in the impure altruism model, because 'an impact philanthropist cannot enjoy saving children if other philanthropists save them first' (p. 2).
10. For a similar model, see Bolton and Ockenfels (2000).
11. For models which introduce other motives like envy and spitefulness, see Fehr and Schmidt (2003).
12. See also Bolton et al. (1998b) and Bolton et al. (2000).
13. This result is replicated in Houser and Kurzban (2003).
14. See also the studies on social interaction effects in general. Individual behaviour has been found to vary with group behaviour, as, for instance, with for criminal activities (Glaeser et al., 1996) and in the case of welfare participation (Bertrand et al., 2000).
15. See also the field experiment by Blumenthal et al. (2001). However, they find no statistically significant effect of informing taxpayers that few others cheat.
16. For studies on the 'identifiable victim effect', see Jenni and Loewenstein (1997) and Small and Loewenstein (2003).
17. A number of studies in psychology analyse how in-group effects can influence the perception of the out-group. Open hostility towards people of the out-group may be the most negative effects of in-group favouritism. For a survey of such intergroup biases, see Hewstone et al. (2002).
18. Communication can also lead to a better understanding of the dilemma structure. The effect of this understanding is ambiguous and is discussed, for example, in Bohnet (1997).

19. A large Swiss charity, for example, raises donations by announcing the donated amount on public radio. The reasons for this technique may be twofold: firstly, people are more willing to donate when others do so as well ('conditional cooperation') and, secondly, it may be easier to express the intention to donate than to actually do it. Surprisingly (for an economist), most people actually donate the promised amount although no enforcement mechanism exists. Cialdini (1993: 57–113) presents many examples of how firms use people's tendency to be consistent with former commitments to sell their products or to raise donations.

20. Interestingly, men and women have different price elasticities: 'when it is relatively expensive to give, women are more generous than men; however as the price of giving decreases, men begin to give more than women' (Andreoni and Vesterlund, 2001: 294). See also Eckel and Grossman (1996b).

21. An exception from this general result is the study by Duncan (1999), who finds that monetary donations and volunteering are substitutes.

22. For a meta-study declaring the crowding effect to be 'a myth', see Eisenberger and Cameron (1996). For an evaluation of the two contradictory meta-studies, see Lepper et al. (1999).

23. For an overview of studies on crowding effects in labour relations with a special focus on pay-for-performance schemes, see Osterloh and Frey (2000).

24. This result is also found in experiments by Fehr and Rockenach (2003) and Fehr and Gächter (2002).

25. However, little is known about whether a motivational crowding-out is due to a change in preferences (Frey, 1997a) or to the perceived nature of the task (Bénabou and Tirole, 2002), or about how exactly intrinsic motivation is rebuilt after an extrinsic incentive is removed.

26. In economics, cooperators are labelled altruists.

27. See also Offerman et al. (1996), who find somewhat lower rates of cooperative subjects.

28. Caplan (2003) discusses the relevance of preference-based explanations for a wide range of economic questions.

29. Because an altruist mimics the behavior of an egoist every time he or she meets one, expectations about others differ between the two types. An egoist believes that everybody is an egoist because he or she only meets people who behave egoistically, while an altruist knows that there are egoists and altruists (Kelley and Stahelski, 1970). For a test of this 'triangle hypothesis', see van Lange (1992).

30. For an overview of virtue ethics, see Almender (2000).

31. The importance of processes for utility is often neglected in economics. For a survey on procedural utility, see Frey et al. (2003).

32. The 'negative-state-relief' theory in psychology (see Cialdini et al., 1982) proposes exactly the opposite: people in a bad mood behave more pro-socially because they think that doing good lifts the bad mood.

PART II

Empirical Analysis

3. Pro-social Behaviour in a Natural Laboratory*

Empirical evidence that people behave pro-socially does exist and initial approaches have been undertaken to explain this deviation from the self-interest hypothesis. However, as shown in Chapter 2, more field evidence is a crucial step towards analysing the conditions under which people behave pro-socially. Such an empirical strategy will increase understanding of what ultimately motivates people to contribute to public goods and enable researchers to test the extent to which behavioural results from the laboratory can be generalized to naturally occurring situations. In the empirical part of this book, pro-social behaviour is analysed using data about contributions to two social funds at the University of Zurich. This data set allows an investigation of pro-social behaviour in a natural laboratory, in which *all* students of the University of Zurich have to decide *each* semester whether they want to contribute to two social funds. As a result, a large panel data set can be exploited analysing contributions to a naturally occurring public good.

In this chapter the data set is introduced and analysed on a descriptive level. The descriptive analysis of the general pattern of contributions allows initial insights into the motivation for pro-social behaviour. The behaviour of the students clearly indicates that people are not solely motivated by self-interest. Even in an anonymous situation, people are willing to contribute positive amounts of money to people who are worse off. Two behavioural patterns are especially interesting in the light of the relative importance of the theories on pro-social behaviour presented in the previous chapter. Firstly, minor changes in the context of the decision have large effects on the contributions to the two funds. In particular, it matters a great deal how students are asked whether they want to donate money. Secondly, the willingness to contribute does not drop off with repetition as dramatically as shown in laboratory experiments. Although there is no possibility of punishing free-riders, contributions do not erode over time. This pattern is interesting in particular when discussing the norm of reciprocity. However, the descriptive analysis is not conclusive and will be complemented with in-

* Some parts of this chapter are based on Frey, Bruno S. and Stephan Meier (2003). Pro-social Behavior in a Natural Setting. *Journal of Economic Behavior and Organizations* 54(1). 65-88. With permission from Elsevier.

depth analyses of particular aspects in later chapters.

Section 3.1 presents the data set for this and the following chapters. The strength and weaknesses of the data set are evaluated and summary statistics are given. Section 3.2 presents a descriptive analysis of the general pattern of contributions to the two funds. Section 3.3 points to the problems of a solely descriptive analysis. This section will then be used to present the two econometric models, which address these problems in a multivariate analysis. As these two models will be used throughout the remainder of the book, Section 3.3 provides a brief excursus into the statistical methods used here. Section 3.4 draws concluding remarks.

3.1   DATA SET ON CONTRIBUTIONS TO TWO SOCIAL FUNDS

3.1.1   Decision Setting

Each semester, every student at the University of Zurich has to decide whether or not he or she wants to contribute to two official social funds in addition to the compulsory tuition fee. On the official form for renewing their registration, students are asked whether they want to voluntarily give a set sum (CHF 7, about €4.7) to a fund which offers low-interest loans to students in financial difficulties (*Loan Fund*) and/or another set sum (CHF 5, about €3.4) to a fund supporting foreigners who study at the University of Zurich (*Foreigner Fund*). Without their explicit consent by marking a box, students do not contribute to any fund at all. Figure 3.1 presents the decision situation, to which students must sign their assent. One month later, the students receive an invoice with the compulsory tuition fee plus the selected amount for the social funds.

Would you like to contribute voluntarily to the following two social funds:

Loan Fund (CHF 7)	☐ Yes	☐ No
Foreigner Fund (CHF 5)	☐ Yes	☐ No

Figure 3.1   Decision to contribute to the two social funds

The decisions of *all* students can be observed for the period from the winter semester 1998/99 up to and including the winter semester 2002/03 (that is, nine semesters). The fact that every student has to decide each semester whether to contribute or not leads to a large number of observations. The giving behaviour of 37,588 students can be observed. They decide on average 4.8 times, depending on how many semesters they have attended. The decisions of the nine periods are pooled, which generates 180,225 observations. Table 3.1 presents the summary statistics of the data set. Students in the data set from freshmen to Ph.D. students are on average around 28 years old and in the tenth semester.

Table 3.1   Summary statistics

Variables	Field data	Survey data
Number of observations	180,225	3,256
Contributions to at least one fund	69.6%	79.7%
Age (mean; s.d.)	27.78 (8.05)	26.66 (5.59)
Aged below 26	47.9%	
Aged 26-30	27.4%	
Aged 31-35	12.7%	
Aged 36-40	6.1%	
Aged above 40	5.8%	
Gender		
Women	50.5%	47.5%
Men	49.5%	52.5%
Nationality		
Foreigner	11.7%	
Swiss	88.3%	
Number of semesters (mean; s.d.)	10.47 (8.21)	6.94 (5.07)
Freshmen	7.6%	
Basic study	22.3%	
Main phase	53.9%	
Ph.D. study	16.2%	
Economics and business students	10.3%	12.9%
Non-economists	89.7%	87.1%
Monthly income in CHF (mean s.d.)		1,372 (1,924)
Percentage earning their own living (mean s.d.)		57.6 (34.7)
Parents pay the tuition fee		45.4%

Source: The data set is compiled from data provided by the accounting department of the University of Zurich, 1998-2002. The survey data is based on my own survey study, 2000.

In addition, an anonymous on-line survey was undertaken among the same student population.[1] The response rate was 18 per cent. From this sample, 3,256 answers could be used, containing responses to all the questions relevant for the context analysed. This sample is not totally representative (not surprisingly, a larger number of economics students responded to the questionnaire sent out by an economist), but with respect to gender and age, the sample approximately corresponds to the distribution of students at the University of Zurich (see Table 3.1 for summary statistics of the survey data set). The survey again asked whether the person contributed money to one or both of the funds. Eighty per cent responded that they did, compared to the 70 per cent who actually contributed. Even taking into account that people in the survey may be in an earlier stage in their studies and therefore more likely to contribute (see Section 2.2 for the effect of repetition), the difference is too large to be explained in this way. The difference between survey answers and actual behaviour is found in many survey-based studies. While the differences can be the result of people lying (see Eichenberger and Oberholzer-Gee, 1998; Bertrand and Mullainathan, 2001 for differences between hypothetical and real decisions), a more convincing explanation is that people who actually contributed to the funds are more likely to respond to the on-line survey. The differences should be kept in mind when interpreting the survey data.

3.1.2   Characteristics of the Data Set

The decision setting of contributions to the University of Zurich's social funds has some special characteristics. They constitute the advantages and also the limits of the data set. The decision situation has at least four features which are advantageous for analysing pro-social behaviour:

1. *Naturally occurring decision situation*   The data set allows the analysis of pro-social behaviour in a naturally occurring decision. In contrast to decisions in the laboratory, subjects contribute to a real public good in a social context. Such field studies on pro-social behaviour are important complements of experimental studies, as has already been argued in the previous chapter. The decision situation includes *all* students from the University of Zurich, which leads to a huge data set. The fact that all students have to decide whether they want to contribute or not avoids the selection problem of the subject pool (Ball and Cech, 1996).
2. *Controlled environment*   The data set allows for a number of factors, which might influence behaviour, to be kept constant. For example, the decision setting is the same for all the students. They are asked in the same way and around the same time each year whether they are willing

to contribute to the two funds. Personal characteristics like age, gender, nationality or field of study can be controlled. It is known, for example, that gender has a positive influence on donations, but women are also less likely to choose economics as their major. If the analysis does not establish controls for gender, any effect of 'being an economics student' could also be a gender effect. In addition, people decide whether or not to contribute many times in a row, and therefore the data set has a panel structure. This makes it possible to control for time-invariant, unobservable personal heterogeneity. Controlling for heterogeneity is important because selection effects (for example, Ph.D. students are a particular selection of people) can be excluded, but also because different 'types' of people may react differently to experimental interventions. For example, people who never contribute to the two funds may not be sensitive to monetary incentives to increase their pro-social behaviour. A within-subject analysis can lead to interesting insights about how preferences revealed by past behaviour (the 'type of person') influences the effect of institutional changes on pro-social behaviour.

3. *Anonymity*   The decision to contribute to the two social funds is made anonymously. Students decide at home and send their decision by mail to the University. The data about who contributes to the funds is only known by the administration of the University and is neither communicated to the greater public nor communicated to the administration of the two funds. This anonymity allows the researcher to exclude motives for giving based on prestige or social pressure. As the administration of the funds does not know the name of the students who contributed, having made a contribution is of course not a prerequisite for receiving financial support from the funds at a later stage.

4. *Repetition*   The decision to contribute to the two funds is repeated every semester. Questions about how people change their behaviour with repetition can be addressed. Repetition is important because most real-life decisions have to be taken more than once and therefore learning effects are possible.

The naturally occurring decision situation does, however, have some limitations. Two features of the decision situation have to be kept in mind when interpreting the results of the analysis:

1. *Only students*   The analysis is by design limited to the pro-social behaviour of students. Aside from the fact that this has various advantages, in particular because students are an intelligent and a quite homogeneous subject pool, the question can be raised whether the results apply to the general population. This book cannot provide an answer.

However, there are indicators that lead one to expect that the students' behaviour is not much different from the behaviour of the general population in a similar decision situation. Students in Zurich normally do not live in students' dormitories but in the city. The exchange with the general population is therefore notable. As a considerable number of the students are at the same time in gainful employment, they also tend to be in close contact with the rest of the population.

2. *Low stakes*   Students decide about the contribution of a small sum of money. Even if some of the students have little money at their disposal, the contributions are much smaller than in other public good situations. It could be argued that in such low-cost decisions, people behave more pro-socially than in high-cost situations (see Diekmann and Preisendörfer, 2003 for survey evidence). However, a large number of situations where people decide to behave pro-socially are in fact low-cost. People seldom have to decide whether they would be willing to heroically rescue another person.[2] In addition, it could be shown in laboratory experiments that stakes are not as important for the operation of fairness norms (Cameron, 1999; Fehr et al., 2002). In these studies it matters little whether people decide about $10 or about an amount equivalent to a monthly salary. Whether this statement also holds for situations similar to the decision at the University of Zurich is an open question. However, the contributions to the two funds can serve as a proxy for more general pro-social behaviour. In the on-line survey, people were asked whether they donate money to other funds (apart from the two social funds) and whether they volunteer. People who contribute to at least one of the two funds are statistically significantly more likely to donate to other funds. 56.5 per cent of people who contribute to the funds also donate to other funds, versus only 48.7 per cent of people who do not contribute to the social funds donating to other charitable funds ($t = 3.56$; $p < 0.001$). Students who contribute to the two funds also donate more money: on average CHF 259.5 (s.d. = 14.4) versus CHF 197.6 (s.d. = 27.3) per year. The difference is statistically significant on the 90 per cent level ($t = 1.87$; $p < 0.06$). In the case of volunteering, the situation is less clear. Students who donate to the two funds volunteer more, but the difference is not statistically significant. However, one can see that the contributions to the two social funds, even if they are small, can indeed act as some sort of proxy for more general pro-social behaviour. In addition, as the amount is similar to the amount used in most experimental studies, the result of the pro-social behaviour in the field can be compared to behaviour in laboratory experiments.

In sum, the panel data set of the University of Zurich offers a unique opportunity to analyse pro-social behaviour in a naturally occurring situation. It includes the decisions of all students at the University and has therefore many advantages over previous studies. These features can provide new insights about pro-social behaviour. In a first step, the decisions of the students are analysed in a descriptive way, deducing general patterns of giving to the two funds. The data set from the contributions to the two social funds is also used in the three chapters that follow, where special aspects of pro-social behaviour are analysed in-depth.

3.2 GENERAL PATTERN OF PRO-SOCIAL BEHAVIOUR: DESCRIPTIVE ANALYSIS

In the descriptive analysis, various aspects of pro-social behaviour will be explored empirically. Firstly, the overall level of contributions to the two funds is presented, along with whether people stick to their first decision. Secondly, the effect of repetition on the willingness to contribute is investigated. Thirdly, framing effects are analysed. Fourthly, I discuss whether identification with the University or a special group in the organization has an impact on giving. And fifthly, I consider whether people differ substantially in their pro-social preferences.

3.2.1 Level of Contribution

The raw data suggest that the students in the sample do not act according to the predictions of the traditional economic model of selfish individuals. A large proportion of the students are prepared to contribute to the funds. Between the years 1998–2002, on average more than 69 per cent of the individuals contributed to at least one of the funds (see Table 3.2). More than 62 per cent contributed to both funds. In dictator game experiments, the contribution of the subjects is normally much smaller. These differences can be explained by the fact that recipients differ. While in dictator games students share money with other students, in the case of the two social funds the money is earmarked for needy students. Eckel and Grossman (1996a) show in an anonymous dictator game that contributions are much larger if the subjects can give money to an established charity rather than to another experimental subject who does not need the money urgently.

Most of the students either always contribute or never contribute to one of the funds. Results from laboratory experiments show that subjects basically tend to divide into two groups: one group who free-rides all the time and another group of subjects who does not. Figure 3.2 shows the distribution of 'types' according to their past behaviour in the total student population. The 'coefficient of past behaviour' indicates the number of previous decision situations in which the subject decided to contribute. This is captured by a coefficient ranging from 0 to 1. Thus, a coefficient of 0.5 indicates that this particular individual contributed in half of the decision situations in which he or she was involved. Almost 50 per cent of the students contributed in all previous decisions to at least one of the funds. Around 10 per cent never contributed to either of the two funds. The rest fall somewhere in between.[3] The fact that a large proportion of the students always contribute in their previous decisions may be an indicator that students keep on contributing even after several rounds.

Table 3.2   Contributions to two social funds, University of Zurich

Contributions to ...	Absolute	%
... both funds (€8.1)	113,420	62.9
... Foreigner Fund only (€3.4)	7,389	4.1
... Loan Fund only (€4.7)	4,686	2.6
... neither of the two funds	54,730	30.4
Total	180,225	100.0

Source: University of Zurich, 1998-2002.

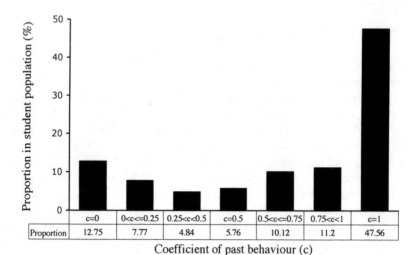

	c=0	0<c<=0.25	0.25<c<0.5	c=0.5	0.5<c<=0.75	0.75<c<1	c=1
Proportion	12.75	7.77	4.84	5.76	10.12	11.2	47.56

Coefficient of past behaviour (c)

Source: University of Zurich, 1998-2002.

Figure 3.2   Distribution of 'types'

The results which show that many people contribute in all their previous decisions and some never contribute can also be explained by the fact that people are heterogeneous in their pro-social preferences. Some people derive high utility from contributing while others would suffer disutility from donating. People at the two ends of this continuum are expected to be less sensitive to minor changes in, for example, the price of donating and therefore do not change their behaviour over time. People in between gain only slight utility from contributing. They are therefore expected to be more sensitive to minor changes in the relative prices. In the field experiments in Chapters 4 and 5, it is shown that people who tend towards indifference about contributing react more to a change in the degree of social comparison and the price of giving.

3.2.2 Repetition

As can be noted from the last section, almost half of the students contribute in all their possible decisions. Therefore, one would expect that with repetition, contributions do not decline much. Figure 3.3 shows that willingness to give money to the social funds is dependent on the number of semesters the students have studied so far at the University. The pattern of contributions shows that the level of contribution only slightly decreases with repetition of the decision. In the absence of any form of punishment, one would expect that with repetition cooperation decreases considerably, as shown by public goods experiments (for example, Fehr and Gächter, 2000a). The results of Figure 3.3 show, however, that even after several rounds, a large number of students act pro-socially in an anonymous decision setting. Even without a punishing mechanism, contributions do not decay to zero with repetition. As the decision is completely anonymous and people decide at home, pro-social behaviour does not seem to be due to an experimenter effect or to some other sort of direct reciprocal reaction, as mentioned by Hoffman et al. (1996). These authors believe that, because anonymity is not completely guaranteed, this can explain the high level of donation in one of their dictator game experiments. Johannesson and Persson (2000), on the other hand, by increasing social distance between dictator and recipients even more, find evidence of non-reciprocal altruism.

The decision situation appears to have no official punishment mechanism by the other students due to complete anonymity or by the University due to the fact that the contribution of the students does not influence any possible future support from the funds in case of need. However, three important remarks have to be made as to why reciprocity cannot be excluded as a motivational factor and why contribution rates do not decay strongly: (1) feedback about the behaviour of others is absent; (2) the decision setting may not be totally anonymous; (3) reciprocity in expectation cannot be excluded. These will each be discussed in turn.

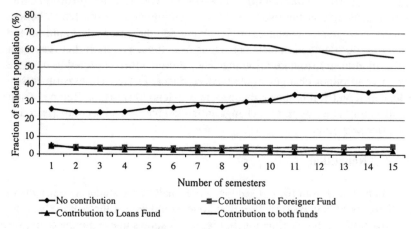

Notes: Students are shown up to their fifteenth semester. Eight semesters, including the exams, is the norm, but 22 per cent of the students study longer.

Source: University of Zurich, 1998-2002.

Figure 3.3   Contributions depending on number of semesters

1. There is no feedback concerning the pro-social behaviour of others in this decision situation. Students do not know how the others behaved in the previous periods, so they cannot update their beliefs. Therefore reciprocity cannot be excluded. According to Fischbacher et al. (2001) such updating of beliefs may lead to a decline in cooperation because, with each successive round, students observe what others contributed and react by giving a little bit less. After several rounds, they find themselves contributing next to nothing. However, a feedback mechanism could have evolved endogenously. But a comparison with others does not seem to be very important for students; if it really were, a student organization would provide the relevant information. There are many real-life public goods where no accurate information about the behaviour of others is available and contribution does not decline over time (an example is tax paying). In other cases, though, there is perfect feedback of aggregate participation rate and no deterioration in cooperation occurs (one example is voting). Houser and Kurzban (2002) show in their public goods game that the decay in cooperation can be explained by a reduction in confusion and that 'it does not seem that

cooperation due to social motives decays much with rounds' (p. 1066). It may be that in the concrete situation analysed here, less confusion is present, reducing the deterioration in cooperation.

2. The decision situation may not be anonymous in two respects. Firstly, other students may apply social pressure. However, Table 3.3 shows the answers to two questions designed to find out whether the students are aware of the behaviour of others and whether they actually talk with each other about the funds. The results indicate that more than three-quarters of the students do not tell their friends whether they contributed or not. Three-quarters of the students never talk with their peers about the funds. Secondly, although the university does keep accounts of who contributes to the funds separate from the administration of the funds, people may still suspect that the University uses the information about the contribution in some kind of way. As in laboratory experiments, such uncertainty can never be ruled out. However, as the relationship to the University administration is quite anonymous and there are no ambiguous signals about the way the information is handled, the probability that persons are sceptical about anonymity is small.

Table 3.3   Knowledge about the contribution of others

Question 1: 'Do your friends know about your contribution?'		
	Absolute	Per cent
No, they do not know	2,568	78.87
Yes, they do know	688	21.13
Total	3,256	100.00
Question 2: 'Do you ever talk about the two social funds to your friends?'		
No, we do not talk	2,488	76.34
Yes, we do talk	771	23.66
Total	3,259	100.00

Source: Own survey; University of Zurich, 2000.

3. Sustaining contributions under anonymity does not exclude reciprocity in expectations ('conditional cooperation'). People may expect others to contribute and react reciprocally to this expectation. Such conditional cooperation may, of course, be due to perceptions of social norms; people indicate how they perceive such norms when asked how many others they expect are contributing. As discussed in the next chapter, however, causality may be the other way round. Given that students do not know for certain what other people do, and that they do not seem particularly interested in the behaviour of other people (as they rarely

talk with their peers about the two social funds), some doubt is cast on the notion that the causal relation between expectations and one's own behaviour comes from any concrete knowledge about the number of overall contributions relative to one's own contribution. A more complete discussion of conditional cooperation as a motive for contributing to the funds is provided in Chapter 4.

To summarize, in the natural decision setting under analysis, pro-social behaviour does not deteriorate dramatically with repetition. This behavioural pattern, occurring as it does in an anonymous situation, does not correspond to many laboratory public good games. As students' knowledge about the behaviour of other students is very limited, this pattern may be due to a lack of feedback about others' behaviour. Another possible explanation for the differences in repetitive behaviour between field and laboratory settings may be identification with the group. As discussed in the next section, identification with the university may increase with repeated registration, an effect which might stabilize contribution to a social fund at the University.

3.2.2 Influence of Institutional Conditions on Pro-social Behaviour

Pro-social behaviour may be dependent on institutional conditions (see the discussion in Chapter 2). Two sorts of particular environmental conditions may be crucial for acquiring contributions to the two social funds and are here analysed empirically: (1) the framing effects of different ways of asking and (2) group identifications. Such context-dependent pro-social behaviour has been labelled 'institutional framing' by Isaac et al. (1991). Bolton et al. (1998a) analyse how much context influences behaviour in dictator games. While they could not detect any experimenter effect, they found that the context of the decision (as given by differences in the written instructions) had a very large impact. This concept of context-dependent pro-social behaviour goes beyond theories of reciprocity and pure altruism.

3.2.3.1 The way of asking
A crucial institutional feature supporting pro-social behaviour is being asked to do so. Moreover, much depends on how one is asked. Different ways of framing the same question institutionally can change the prevalence of pro-social behaviour dramatically (for framing effects see, for example, Lindenberg, 1992; Elliott and Hayward, 1998; Sonnemans et al., 1998; Cookson, 2000).

At the University of Zurich, an exogenous variation of the institutional conditions allows to test the effect on pro-social behaviour. Due to a restructuring of the administration, the University of Zurich changed the official letter for renewing students' registration for the winter semester of 1998. After this semester, the administration was able to handle students' decisions electronically. The students are now asked to contribute in the following way (see Section 1.1 for the decision setting): they have to tick boxes to decide if they want to donate money to one or the other fund, to both or to neither of the funds. One month later, they receive an invoice with the compulsory tuition fee plus the chosen amount for the social funds. Before the winter semester of 1998, students received two invoices and had to choose between the two; one with the amount of the compulsory tuition fee on it, and the other with the amount of the tuition fee *plus* the amount due for contributions to both funds.

Standard economic reasoning would consider the two decisions identical because the underlying decision to be taken is the same: one has to choose whether to contribute money to the two funds or not. The prediction is also identical: a *homo oeconomicus* will *not* donate money in either of the two anonymous decision settings. However, even for non-traditional explanations of cooperative behaviour (for example, reciprocity and pure altruism), the different settings should not affect the behaviour of the subjects. If, for example, cooperation is only conditional on the behaviour of others, no behavioural difference should be observed in the two settings. If framing affects pro-social behaviour in the situation analysed, theories on pro-social behaviour must go *beyond* assumptions of reciprocity or pure altruism because these theories were unable to explain such a result.[4]

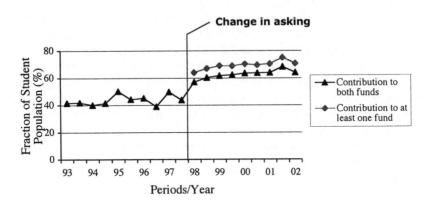

Source. University of Zurich, 1993-2002.

Figure 3.4   Effect of being asked in different ways

Figure 3.4 shows the effect of the exogenous change in the institutional setting on pro-social behaviour. After a change in the way of asking (in the summer semester of 1998), the percentage of people contributing to the two social funds increased from an average of 44 per cent to 62 per cent. The difference is statistically significant (t-value = 11.1, $p < 0.001$). Moreover, in the new system, the students can also opt for only one of the funds, so that the percentage of people who contribute to at least one of the funds saw an even bigger increase. The huge behavioural change due to the framing of the question supports the notion that the institutional condition is crucially important for pro-social behaviour. However, the motivational basis for this dramatic framing effect is unclear. Two possible explanations may be possible.

1. The request process may be perceived as more or less fair, which might increase or decrease the willingness to behave pro-socially. In the new request scheme, students are explicitly asked to contribute and can also opt to contribute to only one of the funds. This explicit asking may be perceived as a fairer procedure compared to the situation where students just received two invoices. A number of studies show that the perceived fairness of various processes can have effects on pro-social behaviour. For example, employees who perceive procedures at work to be fair show more extra-role behaviour (for example, Organ and Ryan, 1995). Frey et al. (2004) review much of the literature on fair procedures and whether procedures are valued as such.
2. Another possible explanation for this result may be that people have 'self-control' problems. 'Self-control' problems can be understood according to O'Donoghue and Rabin (1999) and Laibson (1997), who enhanced a theory by Strotz (1956) of hyperbolic discounting, that people discount costs of events in the far distant future at a higher rate than the same events in the near future. In the decision setting presented above, the costs are the same and have to be paid at almost the same time of the year, but in one setting, the decision to contribute occurs long before the actual payment. Therefore the psychological costs of deciding today and paying in a month's time are lower than deciding today and paying today.

3.2.3.2   Group identification

A second important aspect that influences pro-social behaviour is identification with (1) an organization or (2) a specific group. As has been shown in other studies, especially in studies concerning alumni giving to universities, attachment to an organization is an important factor in explaining donations (Mael and Ashforth, 1992; Clotfelter, 2003). In the case of the contribution to the two social funds at the University of Zurich, changes in the institutional conditions affecting the students' identification with the university should explain some of the variation in giving behaviour.

(1) *Identification with the University*   One such change in the environmental and institutional conditions takes place at the beginning and the end of a student's university life. In both periods, students' actual attendance at the University is lower than in the periods in between. Before taking up their studies (at the very beginning) students obviously have not attended the University at all; at the end of their studies, students no longer attend classes, but prepare for their exams over an extended period of time (more than half a year in the Swiss university system) and therefore attend the University only sporadically. The strongest identification with one's University should exist when students regularly attend courses and feel themselves to be a part of the student body and their *alma mater*. As a consequence, students are expected to contribute significantly less to the social funds at the beginning and end of their studies. As can be seen in Figure 3.3, the donations by freshmen increases after they have spent one semester at the University. While 73 per cent of the freshmen contribute to at least one fund, the contribution rate increases to 76 per cent in the second semester ($t = 4.68$; $p < 0.001$). A similar pattern can be found for people in their last semester. Contribution rates drop to 61 per cent in the last semester, compared to 63 per cent in the next to last semester ($t = 2.36$; $p < 0.05$) and 64 per cent in the semester before that ($t = 4.70$; $p < 0.001$). The descriptive analysis seems to support the positive effect that identification with an organization has on pro-social behaviour.

(2) *Group identification*   Another effect of identification can be analysed for the foreigner fund and whether foreigners are more likely to contribute to this fund. Table 3.4 shows the descriptive statistics for the contributions of foreigners to the social funds. Foreign students, if they contribute at all, mainly tend to support other foreigners. This pattern of pro-social behaviour can be interpreted in the light of the importance of identification for giving. Foreigners identify more with other foreigners. This evidence is consistent with various studies that find that group identity explains a large degree of the variance in pro-social behaviour (Dawes and Thaler, 1988; Simon, 1993; Akerlof and Kranton, 2000). At the University, this group identity is not achieved through discussion, but evolves as an attachment to an anonymous group. This result corresponds to observations that homogeneous communities are more likely to redistribute money from the wealthy to the poor (Alesina and La Ferrara, 2000; Luttmer, 2001).

The empirical results in this section show that pro-social behaviour depends on institutional conditions. Most of all, the way one is asked to contribute to a public good is of great importance, even in the absence of personal contact. Moreover, the results support the crucial effect of identification and identity on giving behaviour.

Table 3.4   Contribution of Swiss and foreigners to the two social funds

Contribution to ...	Swiss		Foreigners	
... both funds	64.31%	(102,336)	52.55%	(11,084)
... Foreigner fund	3.39%	(5,388)	9.49%	(2,001)
... Loan fund	2.74%	(4,357)	1.56%	(329)
... neither of the funds	29.57%	(47,052)	36.40%	(7,678)
Total	100%	(159,133)	100%	(21,092)

Notes: Pearson χ^2 (3) = 2,500.0, $p < 0.01$; number of observations in parentheses.

Source: University of Zurich, 1998-2002.

3.2.4   Heterogeneity in Pro-social Behaviour

People seem to differ in their pro-social preferences, which leads to different behaviour. Some of them free-ride right from the beginning of the game and thus behave according to the standard economic predictions, while others deviate from this prediction substantially and act in a pro-social way. Looking at selection effects may test this notion about different 'types' of people. People with similar preferences may select similar subjects at the University. If this is the case, we should observe that the distribution of selfish types is not random, but systematic.[5] To test this hypothesis, Figure 3.5 looks at the first decision students make to contribute to the two funds. At this time, students have not yet attended any lectures at the University, so any effects resulting from the influence of University training can be excluded. In addition, any effect arising from group interaction is absent due to the fact that students have never met each other before they decide.

While almost 77 per cent of arts students contribute in their first decision to at least one of the funds, only 70 per cent of law students do so. Students of economics seem to be a selection of less pro-socially inclined individuals. In their first decision future economists have a lower contribution rate by nearly 4 percentage points compared to the average. The difference between the students of the various disciplines is remarkable, not least because people go through a very similar high-school system which gives every student basically the same education. The chosen discipline of study, therefore, partially reflects the type of students.

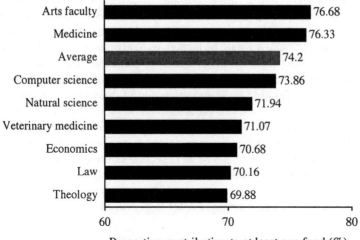

Arts faculty 76.68
Medicine 76.33
Average 74.2
Computer science 73.86
Natural science 71.94
Veterinary medicine 71.07
Economics 70.68
Law 70.16
Theology 69.88

60 70 80

Proportion contributing to at least one fund (%)

Source: University of Zurich, 1998-2002.

Figure 3.5   Contribution rates of freshmen in various disciplines

The result that people group themselves into the various disciplines according to their pro-social preferences will be further studied in Chapter 6. In terms of economics students, one aspect will be central to the analysis: if behavioural differences between economists and non-economists appear in the first semester, then do these differences change during their studies? Looking at the overall contribution rate for the various disciplines shows many changes after the first semester (see Figure 3.A.2 in the Appendix for a respective figure).

3.3   MULTIVARIATE ANALYSIS: AN EXCURSION INTO ECONOMETRICS

The descriptive analysis presented above reveals interesting patterns of pro-social behaviour, such as the fact that contributions to the funds do not fall off as dramatically with repetition (number of semesters) as found in laboratory experiments. The empirical results, however, have to be interpreted with much care because the effects presented can be systematically influenced by third factors. The interpretation of a correlation may then be wrong. For example, as the number of semesters increase, students also become older. It may be that older students are more willing to contribute to the two funds. In this case, age might be the explanation why contributions do not decay much, compared to laboratory experiments where the ten rounds are played in the same afternoon. If the age structure were not taken into consideration, it would be incautious to conclude that contributions do not erode with repetition. Two problems in particular arise if one relies only on descriptive analysis. These problems can be solved using multivariate regression models. Because these models are used throughout the book, in this section I discuss how the two problems can be tackled and I present the two econometric models mainly used here: probit and conditional logit models. The multivariate analyses are explained using the contributions to the two social funds as an example. The next section is therefore the first step towards complementing the results of the descriptive analysis.

3.3.1   Testing for Third Factors: Probit Regressions

In the analytic case of an independent variable affecting a dependent variable, a third variable may influence both variables simultaneously and systematically. Without taking this third variable into account, the effect cannot properly be interpreted. Take, for example, the result that students of the various disciplines differ substantially in their willingness to contribute to the two funds in their first decision. It is possible that students of the various disciplines differ systematically with regard to other characteristics, such as sex or age, that correlate with giving behaviour. This may explain why economics students are less willing to contribute: they are mostly male. In a multivariate regression analysis, all these factors can be taken into account and kept constant.

In the empirical analysis of contributions to the two social funds, the dependent variable often takes the value 1 if students contribute to at least one of the two funds and 0 if students do not contribute at all. The probit model (see Amemiya, 1981) takes into account that the dependent variable is dichotomous. In order to control whether, for example, economists give less because they are male, the following model has to be estimated:

$$\text{Probability (at least one fund} = 1) = \text{Prob}(\beta_1 + \beta_2 * X + \beta_3 * Y + \beta_4 * Z + \varepsilon > 0)$$
$$= 1 - \Phi(-\beta_1 - \beta_2 * X - \beta_3 * Y - \beta_4 * Z)$$

where:	X	vector of faculties,
	Y	vector of demographical variables,
	Z	vector of additional control variables,
	$\beta_{1,2,3,4}$	vector of the estimated coefficients,
	ε	a normally distributed error term,
	$\Phi()$	Standard normal cumulative distribution function.

The log-likelihood function can therefore be written in the following manner:

$$\ln L = \sum_{i, \text{ who contribute}} \ln [1 - \Phi(- x'_i b)] + \sum_{i, \text{ who do not contribute}} \ln \Phi(- x'_i b)$$

The coefficients in a probit model are difficult to interpret. Therefore, marginal effects are computed which indicate how the probability of contributing changes compared to the reference group for dummy variables and how it changes if the independent variables change one unit for all continuous variables. Marginal effects are calculated in the following way:

$$b_i = \frac{\partial \Phi(xb)}{\partial x_i}\bigg|_{x=\bar{x}} = \phi(\bar{x}b)b_i$$

Table 3.5   *Student's contribution in different faculties in the first semester*

Dichotomous dependent variable: 'Contribution to at least one fund' = 1

Arts faculty	Reference group		
Medicine	-0.012	(-0.26)	[0.3%]
Veterinary medicine	-0.149*	(-2.14)	[-5.0]
Natural science	-0.175**	(-4.29)	[-5.9]
Computer science	-0.189*	(-3.16)	[-6.4]
Theology	-0.206	(-1.40)	[-7.0]
Law	-0.208**	(-6.24)	[-7.0]
Economics	-0.240**	(-6.29)	[-8.1]
Control variables			
Age 26-30	0.016	(0.30)	[0.5]
Age 31-35	0.106	(1.26)	[0.3]
Age 36-40	0.195	(1.57)	[5.9]
Aged over 40	0.304*	(2.14)	[8.7]
Gender (female = 1)	-0.154**	(-6.24)	[-4.9]
Nationality (foreigner = 1)	-0.0003	(-0.01)	[-0.0]
Married (= 1)	0.017	(0.19)	[0.6]
Constant	-0.515**	(15.34)	
Period dummies	[Yes]		
Number of observations	13,685		
Log likelihood	-7696.493		

Notes: Coefficient of a probit regression. z-values in parentheses. Marginal effects in brackets. Reference group consists of 'Arts faculty', 'aged below 26', 'male', 'unmarried', 'Swiss', 'semester 1998/99'.
Level of significance: * $0.01 < p < 0.05$, ** $p < 0.01$.

Source: University of Zurich, 1998-2002.

In Table 3.5 a probit model is presented for the first decision to contribute. As *the* first decision is by definition unique, students are represented only once in the estimations. The decisions of 13,685 freshmen are analysed from 1998 until 2002. Apart from the variables for the disciplines, a number of variables control for age, gender, nationality and marital status. A variable for the time period controls for the respective year.

The results in Table 3.5 support the hypothesis that students differ in their social preferences and select along these preferences into different disciplines. As in the descriptive analysis, the differences between the disciplines remain. For example, the willingness of economists to contribute to at least one of the funds is *ceteris paribus* 8 percentage points lower than the reference group ($p < 0.01$). The control variables show that *age* has only a minor effect on the first decision. For people below 40, age cannot explain contributions to the two funds. *Women* tend to contribute substantially less in the first semester than men. The probability of women contributing is almost 5 percentage points lower than for men. *Nationality* and *marital status* have no statistically significant influence on the contribution to the two funds. The regression in Table 3.5 is limited to the first semester and is therefore a cross-sectional analysis. To illustrate the second empirical problem evolving in this book, the next section looks at overall contributions to the two social funds.

3.3.2 Unobservable Individual Heterogeneity: Conditional Logit Model with Individual Fixed Effects

In Panel I of Table 3.6 another probit regression is presented with the decisions of all students. The decisions are pooled, which leads to 156,841 observations.[6] The results from identification with the University are supported in a multivariate regression; the probability that a first-semester student will contribute money is 1.8 percentage points lower than those in the following semesters (the reference period is the *basic* study). This effect is statistically significant at the 99 per cent level. The effect on contributing by students in the last semester is also shown in Table 3.6. The variable for the last semester takes the value 1 if a student is in his or her last semester and 0 otherwise. The probability of contributing to at least one fund decreases by 7 percentage points in the last semester compared to the preceding periods. The two behavioural regularities observed – that students tend to contribute less before they start their studies and at the very end of their studies – is consistent with a changing identification with the University as an organization.

A problem with probit models is constituted by unobservable time-invariant heterogeneity. Such factors may systematically influence the dependent and independent variables of a probit model. If these factors are not taken into account, the coefficients of a probit model can lead to false conclusions. For example, Ph.D. students constitute a selection of people which differ from first-degree students in terms which might be important for pro-social behaviour. This is most obvious in the case of business administration: people who enter the Ph.D. study probably differ from students who enter a consulting firm directly after their master's degree. It could well be that the former are more pro-socially inclined. To exclude the possibility that unobservable differences between students systematically influence the results, one should observe a future Ph.D. student during his or her first degree and analyse whether entering the Ph.D. study has influenced his or her pro-social behaviour. Conditional logit models with individual fixed effects take this time-invariant unobservable heterogeneity into account (see Greene, 1997: 896-901).

The function of individual heterogeneity can be written:

$$Y_{it} = f\left(X_{it}\beta + \alpha_i + \varepsilon_{it}\right)$$

where Y is an action of individual i at time t. This action (for example contributing to at least one fund) is a function of various variables X and a time-invariant individual constant term α. The error term is ε. This estimation for a dichotomous dependent variable Y cannot be made in a probit model, but in a logit model. It appears as:

$$\text{Prob}\,(y_{it} = \text{contribute}) = \frac{e^{\alpha_i + b'x_{it}}}{1 + e^{\alpha_i + b'x_{it}}}$$

In order to estimate this fixed-effects logit function, the following conditional likelihood function is used:

$$L^c = \prod_{i=1}^{n} \text{Prob}\left(Y_{i1} = y_{i1}, Y_{i2} = y_{i2}, \dots, Y_{iT} = y_{iT} \,\middle|\, \sum_{t=1}^{T} y_{it}\right)$$

For people who change their behaviour y at least once, probabilities can be received where the individual constant term a_i drops out of the likelihood function (see Greene, 1997: 900, for details). The intuition behind this is that if one knows how often people contributed ($y = 1$), one can use this as a condition for calculating the coefficient β. The individual constant term a_i determines the overall proportions of 1s (how often people contributed) in the data. The other variables (Xs) and the coefficients (βs) determine *when* those contributions occur. The estimations of β are then independent of the individual heterogeneity a_i.

The conditional logit model applies only to people who have a variation in the dichotomous dependent variable, that is who have changed their behaviour at least once. From those who did not change their behaviour, nothing can be learnt in such a framework. This explains why in Panel II of Table 3.6, the number of observations dropped to 60,522. In contrast to the probit model, the model with personal fixed effects uses the panel structure of a data set and estimates the effect of a change in the independent variable on the dependent variable *within* subjects. The model takes a different constant term for every individual, which explains why no constant term is computed for Panel II. For the conditional logit model it is also not possible to estimate marginal effects.

The conditional logit model with individual fixed effects supports the view that people contribute less in the first and the last semester at the University. The effects are statistically significant at the 99 per cent level. This is consistent with the notion that identification is important for the behaviour of students. The statistically significant effect of entering the main stage is also consistent with higher identification with the University.

The control variables in Table 3.6 show the expected results. As could already be seen in the descriptive statistics (see Figure 3.3), the *Number of semesters* attended decreases the probability of a contribution to the funds, but not dramatically so. *Gender* has an effect on giving behaviour. The probability that women will contribute to the funds is 0.6 percentage points lower than it is for men in the probit model. This result contradicts previous results for behavioural differences between women and men (Eckel and Grossman, 1997; Ortmann and Tichy, 1999). The fact that the amount of money involved is relatively low may explain these differences, as men are found to be more pro-socially active when the price is low, while women tend to be more pro-socially active when prices are relatively high (Andreoni and Vesterlund, 2001). The results of the field experiment presented in Chapter 5, however, do not support this statement. The probability that *foreign* students will contribute to the social funds is smaller than for Swiss students. *Married* students are more generous than their single colleagues; however, the effect is not statistically significant in a fixed-effects model. Marriage itself does not make one more generous, but married students are a special selection.[7] Over time, the willingness to contribute increases, as indicated by the period dummies.

In sum, the two multivariate models presented help to overcome problems with the descriptive analysis and make the interpretation of correlations more accurate. In the following empirical chapters, both models will be used to eliminate the systematic influence of third factors as well as the bias of unobservable heterogeneity on results. However, a third problem still remains: the question of causality. The multivariate regressions cannot be conclusive about causality. In the empirical part, exogenous interventions in a field experiment and a natural experiment will address the causality problem. The experimental designs will be discussed in the relevant chapters.

Table 3.6   Contribution to the social funds

Dichotomous dependent variable: 'Contribution to at least one fund' = 1

Variable	Panel I			Panel II	
Freshmen	-0.051** (-3.15)		[-1.8%]	-0.276**	(-6.07)
Basic study	Reference group				
Main phase	0.122** (12.96)		[4.2]	0.156**	(3.67)
Ph.D.	0.016	(1.18)	[0.6]	-0.047	(-0.52)
Last semester	-0.193** (-16.89)		[-7.0]	-0.211**	(-5.49)
Number of semesters	-0.041** (-26.90)		[-1.4]	-0.171**	(-4.80)
(Number of semesters)^2	0.001** (15.98)		[0.02]	0.002**	(4.73)
Control variables					
Age 26-30	0.008	(0.84)	[0.2]	-0.154**	(-3.41)
Age 31-35	0.173** (12.46)		[5.8]	-0.039	(-0.47)
Age 36-40	0.314** (17.25)		[10.1]	-0.033	(-0.24)
Age over 40	0.514** (25.32)		[15.4]	0.062	(0.30)
Gender (female = 1)	0.017*	(-2.52)	[-0.6]		
Nationality (foreigner = 1)	-0.118** (-11.40)		[-4.2]		
Married (= 1)	0.050** (4.15)		[1.7]	0.059	(0.58)
Period 2 (summer semester 1999)	0.083** (6.15)		[2.9]	0.358**	(7.28)
Period 3	0.142** (10.83)		[4.8]	0.563**	(7.52)
Period 4	0.142** (10.56)		[4.8]	0.607**	(5.70)
Period 5	0.178** (13.55)		[6.0]	0.732**	(5.33)
Period 6	0.165** (12.28)		[5.6]	0.752**	(4.40)
Period 7	0.184** (14.17)		[6.2]	0.837**	(4.13)
Period 8	0.322** (23.78)		[10.4]	1.424**	(6.02)
Constant	0.596** (44.12)				
Number of observations	156,841			60,522	
Log likelihood	-94,596.321				

Notes: Panel I shows coefficient of a probit regression. Panel II shows coefficient of a conditional logit model. Reference group consists of 'basic study', 'aged below 26', 'male', 'Swiss', 'Period 1 (semester 1998/99)'. z-values in parentheses. Marginal effects in brackets. *Level of significance.* * $0.01 < p < 0.05$, ** $p < 0.01$.

Source: University of Zurich, 1998-2002.

3.4   CONCLUSION

This chapter has investigated the general pattern of pro-social behaviour by empirically analysing contributions to two social funds at the University of Zurich. After evaluating the advantages and disadvantages of the data set, a descriptive analysis was presented which was complemented with a section on multivariate regression models.

The behaviour of the students is consistent with previous research results showing that people deviate from the self-interest hypothesis. A substantial number of students are prepared to act in a pro-social manner in a naturally occurring and anonymous decision situation. The descriptive analysis furthermore provided three key insights about the conditions for pro-social behaviour in a natural laboratory. The findings allow some initial speculations about the relative importance of the theories presented in Chapter 2. All three findings of the descriptive analysis will be extended with further empirical investigations in the following three chapters.

1. Even after several rounds, a large number of students are willing to behave pro-socially. The decay in contribution is therefore not as severe as that found in previous public goods games. A possible reason may be that the decision situation differs from a pure public good game in two respects. Firstly, the interdependence of payoffs is not as salient as in laboratory experiments, because many more people are involved and the utility people get from the two funds is indirect; secondly, students receive no feedback about the behaviour of others. This may be important in explaining why pro-social behaviour is stable over time. The descriptive analysis is silent about the question of how people would react to such feedback. It is possible that people would behave reciprocally, that is that people would increase their contributions when informed that many others were doing so as well. It is equally possible that if people realized that many others already supported the charity, they would see no need to continue contributing themselves. In the next chapter, the question of whether people's pro-social behaviour is dependent on the behaviour of others will be analysed in a field experiment.

2. Institutional conditions are crucially important for pro-social behaviour. The contributions to the two funds have been found to be very sensitive to framing effects. The design of the way people are asked to contribute is of great importance, in this case resulting in a huge increase in contributions due to a small change in the manner of request. This increase cannot be explained by theories of altruism or reciprocity. However, the mechanisms underlying the effect of the institutional

condition are far from being conclusively explained. Nonetheless, the fact alone that institutional conditions are of great importance when looking at the magnitudes legitimizes the claim that much more effort should be invested in understanding the influence of institutional conditions on pro-social behaviour.

As institutions often influence the relative prices of a decision setting, Chapter 5 investigates the behavioural reaction to a matching mechanism. In the field experiment undertaken, the costs to contribute to the two funds remain the same but the contributions are matched by an anonymous donor. The benefit of an individual donation, therefore, is changed.

3. The analysis of the contribution rates of students from different faculties shows huge differences. One possible explanation may be that people have heterogeneous pro-social preferences and select themselves into different faculties. As the economics faculty in particular is often accused of eroding the citizenship behaviour of its students by stressing the self-interest hypothesis too much, Chapter 6 analyses in depth the relationship between (an economics) education and pro-social behaviour.

NOTES

1. The on-line questionnaire is reproduced at www.iew.unizh.ch/grp/frey/fragebogen.htm.
2. As the research on rescuers of Jews in Nazi Europe shows, ordinary people are prepared to help strangers in situations where the costs involve risking one's life (Oliner and Oliner, 1992).
3. The distribution of types presented may be biased because people differ in the number of decisions taken. In Figure 3.A.1 in the Appendix, people are divided after precisely four decisions, which results in five different types. It can again be shown that most students contributed in all of the four decisions.
4. Andreoni (1992) presents evidence that positive framing leads to more cooperation in a public good experiment than negative framing of the same decision. He explains this difference in the light of the 'warm glow' effect: 'it must be that people enjoy doing a good deed more than they enjoy not doing a bad deed' (p. 11).
5. Similarly, Ockenfels and Weimann (1999) compare the preferences of East and West Germans in laboratory experiments and find differences in their cooperative behaviour.
6. The number of observations in the probit model deviates from the total number of observations in the data set because the variable *last semester* can only be constructed up to the next-to-last semester. Therefore, the observations for period 9 could not be used in the presented specification.
7. For a detailed discussion about selection effect and marriage and how these problems can be answered by using panel data, see Stutzer and Frey (2003c).

APPENDIX

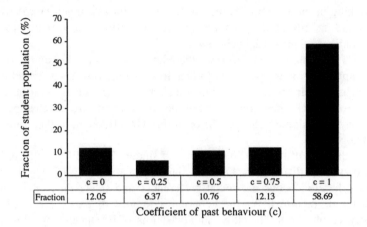

Source: University of Zurich, 1998-2002.

Figure 3.A.1   Distribution of 'types' after four decisions

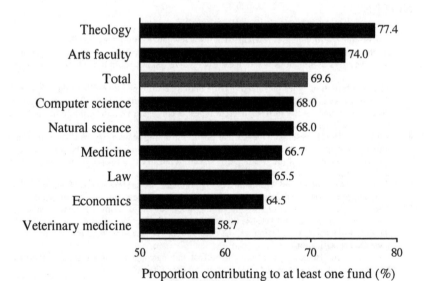

Source: University of Zurich, 1998-2002.

Figure 3.A.2   Differences between disciplines (all semesters)

4. Social Comparisons and Pro-social Behaviour: A Field Experiment[*]

In deciding whether to cooperate in a social dilemma situation, people may care about the pro-social behaviour of the other people involved. People may be willing to contribute to a public good if they know that other people are doing so as well. But if the average individual of a group does not behave pro-socially, a single member of this group may also not be prepared to contribute. This relationship between social comparisons and pro-social behaviour, so-called conditional cooperation, is not trivial because it stands in contrast to standard economic theory and also to pure altruism theories. If people behave according to pure altruism theories, they reduce their own contribution when informed that the others are already contributing.

Testing conditional cooperation faces various difficulties. A positive correlation between an individual's behaviour and the average group behaviour can have at least two potential origins: either the reference group's behaviour influences the behaviour of the individual or the group is constituted by individuals of similar (unobservable) characteristics. Group behaviour in the latter case does not influence individual behaviour, but rather the similar characteristics are responsible for the positive correlation.[1] Further, it is not sufficient to compare one's expectations about the behaviour of others with one's own behaviour. Even if the correlation between expectations and one's own behaviour is positive, causality is not clear. Expectations about others do not necessarily trigger behaviour; sometimes behaviour influences expectations. Such a 'false consensus' effect (for example, Ross et al., 1977) can occur because cooperative people may model their expectations about other peoples' behaviour on their own behaviour, or they may want to justify their own behaviour.

The challenges to measuring conditional cooperation can be addressed if beliefs about the behaviour of the reference group can be experimentally manipulated. Only a few studies, however, explicitly test conditional cooperation in laboratory experiments (see Chapter 2 for a survey of the results). This chapter presents one of the first studies to test 'conditional

[*] This chapter is based on Frey, Bruno S. and Stephan Meier (2004). Social Comparison and Pro-Social Behavior: Testing Conditional Cooperation in a Field Experiment. *American Economic Review* 94(5). 1717-22.

cooperation' for charitable giving outside the laboratory.

After the presentation of the design of the field experiment, in Section 4.2 the behavioural hypothesis is derived based on the theoretical consideration in Chapter 2. In Section 4.3 the effect of the field experiment is analysed and the results presented. In Section 4.4 conclusions are drawn for economic theory and policy.

4.1   DESIGN OF FIELD EXPERIMENT

The field experiment was implemented in the naturally occurring decision situation at the University of Zurich. In the experimental intervention, 2,500 subjects of the student population were selected at random and provided with additional information about the two funds. With the official letter for renewing registration and deciding whether to contribute to the two funds (for the winter semester 2002/3), the administration supplied the students selected with differing information about the behaviour of other students. The sheet of paper that the various treatment groups received differed only with respect to the exact information given (see Figure 4.A.1 in the Appendix for a sample information sheet). Due to the 'institutional difference' that freshmen have to pick up, the registration form at the counter of the administration office, only those students who have already registered and therefore decided at least once in the past are included in the treatment groups. All other non-freshmen constitute the control group.[2] As some students decided not to renew their registration, the decisions of the remaining 2,185 subjects in the field experiment could be observed.

The main part of the field experiment provides the students with information about the behaviour of others. One thousand students were provided with the information that a relatively *high* percentage of the student population (64 per cent) had contributed to the two funds in the past (Treatment 'High'), and another 1,000 students were provided with the information that a relatively *low* percentage (46 per cent) had contributed to the two social funds (Treatment 'Low'). No deception was used; the information is based on real contribution rates, but refers to different time periods. The higher contribution rate applies to the winter term 2001/02. The lower contribution rate indicates the average over the last 10 years.[3] As some of the subjects did not renew their registration, just under 1,000 subjects in each treatment were observed.

In addition to these two basic treatments, an 'expectation' treatment was included in the experiment. For an additional group of 500 students, the expectations were elicited about the behaviour of others by asking them to guess how many other students (as a percentage of the total student population) contributed to *both* of the funds. The students could return the sheet indicating their expectations free of charge by putting it into the official envelope provided by the University administration. There were monetary incentives for the students to give their truly best guess: the estimate closest to the real contribution rate earned a voucher for music or books valued at CHF 100 (about €65), and there was a cinema voucher valued at CHF 20 (about €13) for the five next best guesses. From the eight students who guessed the correct amount (67 per cent) the six winners of the vouchers were selected randomly. Of the 431 students in this treatment who decided to renew their registration, 250 made guesses. This constitutes a return rate of 58.0 per cent, which is high for a 'questionnaire'. People who contribute to the funds are more likely to return the sheet. However, the selection effect is only a minor problem as the level of contribution is not of interest in this chapter, but rather the correlation between expectations about others' behaviour and one's own behaviour. The assumption is made that the correlation also holds for people who did not make any guess.

Table 4.1   Summary statistics for winter term 2002/03

		Treatments		
	Control	'High'	'Low'	'Expectation'
Number of observations	16,957	878	876	250
Number of semesters	11.564	11.530	11.406	10.032
	(8.338)	(7.973)	(8.289)	(7.124)
Age	28.228	27.698	27.887	26.88
	(7.289)	(6.819)	(6.787)	(6.537)
Gender (Female = 1)	51.6%	49.3%	51.6%	52.0%
Coefficient of past	0.732	0.738	0.748	0.746
behaviour	(0.358)	(0.358)	(0.353)	(0.365)

Notes: Standard deviations in parentheses.

Source: Field experiment, University of Zurich, winter term 2002/03.

Table 4.1 shows the summary statistics for the control group and the treatment group. As the assignment was random, no significant differences emerged between the characteristics of subjects in the treatment group 'High' and 'Low' and the rest of the student population. People who made guesses about the behaviour of others are slightly younger than the control group.

Students decide anonymously at home about whether to contribute to the two social funds, but with different information about other students' behaviour at their disposal. The analysis concentrates on contributions to at least one of the funds, although students have to decide whether or not to give to two different funds. Whether people contribute to at least one fund or not is used as a dependent variable, firstly, because most students contribute either to both funds or do not contribute at all (see Chapter 3); secondly, because the results do not change when other dependent variables are included; and thirdly, because it constitutes the lower limit of contribution.

The field experiment has two clear advantages over previous studies:

1. For at least two decades, laboratory experiments have challenged the standard economic assumption. While experimental research leads to many insights about the basics of human behaviour, it is still unclear exactly how these results can be generalized outside the laboratory situation. Field experiments aim to narrow this gap by looking at naturally occurring decision settings, while still controlling for relevant variables.
2. Due to the panel structure of the data set, pro-social preferences, as revealed by past behaviour can be included in the analysis. This makes it possible to identify how different 'types' of people react to social comparison. To analyse such a question with revealed behaviour has advantages over questionnaire-based approaches.

4.2　BEHAVIOURAL HYPOTHESES

According to the theory of conditional cooperation, social comparison in this field situation should lead to higher contribution rates when students are presented with the information that many others have contributed. This prediction is not trivial: if students were to behave according to pure altruism theories (for example, Clotfelter, 1997: 34-5; Croson, 1998), they would reduce their own contribution when informed that other students are already contributing.

The hypothesis to be tested in this chapter predicts that people react positively to the behaviour of others. No one likes being the only one who contributes to a good cause and no one likes being the 'sucker' who is being 'free-ridden' by others. The most distinctive prediction of such a theory is that individual i's probability of contribution increases when the percentage of individuals j ($j = 1, ..., n; j \neq i$) who contribute increases within a given group.

CONDITIONAL COOPERATION HYPOTHESIS: People's pro-social behaviour is conditional on the behaviour of others. The individual behaviour varies positively with the average behaviour in the group. Therefore, the probability of subjects contributing to the social funds in treatment 'High' is expected to be greater than subjects in treatment 'Low'.

ALTRUISM HYPOTHESIS: Altruists will free-ride on the contribution of others. Therefore the probability of subjects contributing in treatment 'High' is expected to be lower than subjects in treatment 'Low'.

The conditional cooperation hypothesis is based on a broad notion of social comparison (see Chapter 2). The idea that the more others contribute, the more one gives, may be based on various motivational reasons: firstly, people may want to behave in a way appropriate to conforming to a social norm; secondly, people may have some sort of fairness preferences such as inequity aversion or a norm of reciprocity; or thirdly, contributions by others may serve as a signal for the quality of the public good, or for the organization which provides the good in the end (for example a charity).

People may be heterogeneous in their reaction to social comparison. If this is the case, two different sorts of heterogeneity may be important for the analysis of the results:

1. Only certain 'types' of people are sensitive to the behaviour of others. While some persons vary their behaviour according to the average behaviour in the group, others are not strongly affected by the behaviour of others. Glaeser et al. (1996) show in their study of social interaction effects on criminal behaviour that some people are not influenced by the behaviour of others, the so-called 'fixed agents'. If people have strong preferences for contributing or not contributing to a good cause, social interaction is unimportant, as opposed to people who do not have such a strong preference either way. This reasoning compares with results from laboratory experiments where a substantial number of the subjects behave completely selfishly, while others show some sort of pro-social preferences.

2. An alternative form of heterogeneity assumes that everybody reacts to the behaviour of others, but people are heterogeneous with respect to the threshold at which they alter their own behaviour. Whereas certain people will begin to cooperate when they realize that a small minority does so, others only cooperate when they know that a large majority is already involved. As the experimental intervention induces beliefs about contribution rates of 46 per cent and 64 per cent, only people who have a threshold in between these boundaries are expected to react to the experimental intervention.

Both aspects of heterogeneity lead to the expectation that only a small fraction of people will react to the experimental intervention. And although the 'types' are randomly distributed over the two treatment groups, it is important to control for unobservable heterogeneity in order to isolate the effect of social comparison.

In the following section, the hypotheses are tested in four steps. Firstly, the relationship between expectations and behaviour is presented. Secondly, the effect of the field experiment on contribution rates is reported. Thirdly, the magnitude of the effect is compared with the correlation between expectations and willingness to contribute, leading to an analysis of heterogeneous reactions to the treatments. Fourthly, the sensitivity of the effect to framing the number of cooperators as the number of free-riders is investigated.

4.3   ANALYSIS AND RESULTS

4.3.1   Own Behaviour and Expectations About Others' Behaviour

In a first step, I analysed whether the reported expectations about the behaviour of others and one's own behaviour correlate positively. On average, students expect 57 per cent of their fellow students to contribute to both social funds (see Figure 4.1 for the distribution of expectations), thus underestimating the real contribution rate of 67 per cent of the students.

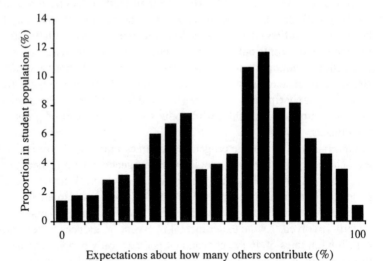

Expectations about how many others contribute (%)

Source: Field experiment, University of Zurich, winter term 2002/03.

Figure 4.1   Distribution of expectations

This result is in line with other studies, which find that people generally underestimate the extent of pro-social behaviour (for evidence on tax compliance, see Wenzel, 2001). However, the interesting question is whether expectations have an influence on one's own pro-social behaviour, which is assumed to be independent of the level of expectations.

The result of the correlation between expectations and one's own behaviour shows that the higher the expectation of the students about the average group behaviour, the more likely it is that these students will contribute to at least one fund. The coefficient of correlation between the expectations expressed and the contribution to at least one fund is 0.34 ($p < 0.001$). Figure 4.2 plots the contribution rate and the expectations (grouped in increments of 5 percentage points from $0 \leq x < 5$ per cent to $95 \leq x \leq 100$ per cent, which leads to 20 groups). The figure shows that the positive effect is substantial. The vector of the marginal effect in a probit analysis is 0.0062 (the estimation is reproduced in Panel II of Table 4.3). A change in the perceived cooperation rate of others by 10 percentage points, evaluated at the mean expectation, raises the probability of contributing by more than 6 percentage points. This result corresponds with the results of various laboratory studies. However, as discussed above, causality is not clear. A 'false consensus' effect may be at work, where people project their own behaviour onto others.[4] It is therefore important to experimentally induce beliefs in order to analyse how people react when they are presented with the relatively 'High' or 'Low' contribution rates.

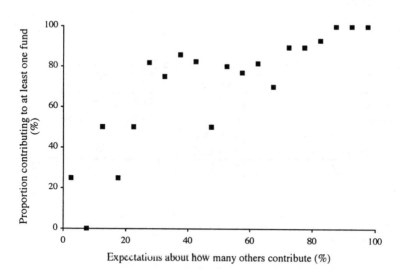

Source: Field experiment, University of Zurich, winter term 2002/03.

Figure 4.2   Correlation between expectations and behaviour

4.3.2   Behavioural Responses to High or Low Contribution Rate

In a second step, I analysed whether people adapt their behaviour when presented with a relatively 'High' or 'Low' contribution rate on the part of others. The results of the field experiment are consistent with the hypothesis that people are partly driven by conditional cooperation: the probability of students contributing correlates positively with the mean contribution rate in the reference group. The percentage of students contributing to at least one of the funds increases more than 2.5 percentage points when they receive the information that 64 per cent of others have contributed, compared to the group who learns that only 46 per cent do so. But the difference is not statistically significant at a conventional level (t-value $= 1.199$, $p < 0.231$). However, such a result may be due to heterogeneity in people's preferences. Some students derive high utility from contributing and others presumably would suffer disutility if they had to contribute. As the decision is censored to either contributing or not contributing, those who have always given or never given should not be substantially affected by social comparison. Students whose utility gain is somewhere between the extremes should be more likely to respond. To control for such individual heterogeneity, a conditional logit model was calculated with individual fixed effects. The average effect, therefore, is not very representative and its estimation comes with a large standard error.

Table 4.2   Reaction to the behaviour of others

Dichotomous dependent variable: Contribution to at least one fund ($= 1$)

Variable	Coefficient	z-value	$p > |z|$
Treatment 'High' (64%)	0.401**	(3.00)	0.003
Treatment 'Low' (46%)	-0.025	(-0.19)	0.851
Individual fixed effects	included		
Semester dummies	included		
Number of observations	70,269		
Log likelihood	-26,451.239		

Notes: Test of differences for treatment 'High' - 'Low' = 0.0: $\chi^2(1) = 5.44$, $p < 0.0197$. Conditional logit model with individual fixed effects. z-values in parentheses. *Level of significance*: * $0.01 < p < 0.05$, ** $p < 0.01$.

Source: Field experiment, University of Zurich, winter term 2002/03.

Table 4.2 presents the conditional logit model, where the dependent variable takes the value 1 when the subject decides to contribute to at least one fund, and 0 otherwise. Individual fixed effects and time dummies are incorporated. The control group consists of all students not in the treatment groups who have already decided at least twice; freshmen are thus excluded. The model can therefore test the effect of being in one of the two treatments and whether differences between the two treatments emerge.

The results of Table 4.2 support the conditional cooperation hypothesis: people who are presented with a high contribution rate are more likely to contribute than people who are told that not as many others have contributed to the funds. A χ^2-test of differences between the two coefficients for the two treatments shows that they are statistically significant at a 95 per cent level ($\chi^2(1) = 5.44$, $p < 0.0197$). The difference in behaviour due to the behaviour of others is substantial, especially if one takes into account the specific features of the naturally occurring decision setting. Firstly, as the experimental intervention is based on *actual* contribution rates, no extreme cooperation rates were induced. The difference between 46 per cent and 64 per cent of students contributing is relatively modest compared to past laboratory studies where people are confronted with extreme cases, such as zero contribution rates (see for example, Weimann, 1994). The results therefore provide even stronger support for 'conditional cooperation'. Secondly, the students face a dichotomous decision (whether to contribute or not). This leaves little room for marginally adjusting one's behaviour. To take as the dependent variable the amount paid to the funds – which can take the value CHF 0, 5, 7 or 12, depending on the students' choice to contribute to both, neither, or only one specific fund – does not change the results (see Table 4.A.1 in the Appendix for results on contributions to both funds). Thirdly, none of the subjects are contributing for the first time, so contributing may have become a kind of habit, where social comparison may lose some importance. Thus, the results from the field experiment show that, even in a naturally occurring situation, people react to relatively small changes in the cooperation rate of others.

Table 4.2 also shows that people react in an *asymmetrical way* to the induced 'High' or 'Low' cooperation rates. Students *increase* their willingness to contribute when presented with many others doing so. This difference is statistically significant at the 99 per cent level. But they do *not decrease* their willingness when only a few others contribute. Although the difference bears the expected sign, it is not statistically significant. This result is surprising, because one may have expected that people would hate being in the minority of those behaving pro-socially while others free-ride. The results of the field experiment show that people mimic the behaviour of free-riders far less often than can be assumed, while they behave pro-socially if they see that many others do the same. However, it may well be that people's willingness to contribute decreases if less than the experimentally induced 46 per cent of the whole student population contributes.

To go into greater detail, the next section addresses the question of who is in fact most sensitive to the behaviour of others.

4.3.3   Who is Sensitive to the Behaviour of Other Persons?

One may well expect that not all individuals behave in a cooperative way conditional on the behaviour of others. Numerous studies find individual heterogeneity among pro-social preferences, and therefore in cooperative behaviour, in social dilemma situations. Glaeser et al. (1996) explicitly incorporate different 'types' of person into their model of social interactions. The 'fixed agents' do not react to other people's behaviour in specific situations; their specific decisions are 'far too certain' to allow themselves to be affected by others. Other individuals' decisions are uncertain, however, and they are therefore more easily influenced by the average behaviour in the reference group. In the case of the decision setting at the University of Zurich, it is useful to consider heterogeneous pro-social preferences. People with weak preferences about contributing to the two funds are not expected to be very sensitive to the minor change in the contribution rate of the group. People with strong preferences about contributing are also expected not to be much affected. For people in between these extreme preferences, the behaviour of others may be more decisive.

In other studies, the various types are detected by looking at how many people actually behave in a conditionally cooperative way in a laboratory experiment that test conditional cooperation. Here a different approach is used to obtain a proxy for the type of subjects.[5] In the panel data set, past behaviour is used as a proxy for the pro-social preferences. People who never contributed, or those who always contributed when they had a chance to do so, are expected to react more like 'fixed agents' than people who seem to be more uncertain and have changed their behaviour at least once. The coefficient of past behaviour indicates the fraction of previous decision situations in which the subject decided to contribute. This is reflected by a coefficient ranging from 0 to 1. Accordingly, a coefficient of 0.5 indicates that this particular individual contributed in half of the decision situations in which he or she was involved (see Chapter 3 for a detailed description). The subjects who are more indifferent with regard to contributing are expected to be more sensitive to the induced beliefs.

Panel I in Table 4.3 controls for this past behaviour. The dependent variable is 1 if students contributed to at least one of the funds, and is 0 otherwise. The probit model incorporates only students who were subjects of one of the two treatments. The effect of the treatment 'High' (64 per cent) is compared to the reference treatment in which students received the information that few others (46 per cent) contributed (treatment 'Low'). This procedure is chosen in order to isolate the pure effect of the information that many or few others contribute. As students of both treatment groups received an additional sheet of paper from the University, the two treatment groups differ only in the information received. As the coefficients of a probit analysis are not easy to interpret, the computed marginal effect shows how the probability of contributing changes compared to the reference group.

The results of the conditional logit model support the claim that people contribute *ceteris paribus* more to the two funds when many others do so as well. The effect is statistically significant at the 99 per cent level. The marginal effect of 4.6 percentage points is large when taking into account that the decision does not leave much room for reaction and the intervention is not strong.

Table 4.3   Conditional cooperation controlling for past behaviour

Dichotomous dependent variable: Contribution to at least one fund (=1)

Variable	Panel I	Panel II	Panel III
Treatment 'High' (64%)	0.180**		
	(2.20)		
	[4.6%]		
Treatment 'Low' (46%)	Reference group		
Elicited expectations		0.0215**	0.0128*
		(5.17)	(2.31)
		[0.6%]	[0.3%]
Coefficient of past behaviour	2.721**		2.821**
	(24.30)		(8.95)
	[69.1%]		[63.8%]
Constant	-1.162**	-0.414	-1.759**
	(-12.59)	(-1.79	(-5.18)
Number of observations	1,754	250	250
Log likelihood	-594.284	-122.026	-70.237

Notes: Coefficients of probit regressions. z-value in parentheses; marginal effects in brackets. *Level of significance:* * $0.01 < p < 0.05$, ** $p < 0.01$.

Source: Field experiment, University of Zurich, winter term 2002/03.

Table 4.3 also shows that past behaviour is indeed an important determinant of behaviour and may capture the heterogeneous preferences for contributing to the funds. A number of people have a strong preference for contributing to the two funds and their decision to contribute is relatively stable – over time as well.

The change from an induced cooperation rate of 46 per cent to 64 per cent can be compared to a change in the elicited expectation of the same magnitude. How much does the probability of contributing change when students either believe that 46 per cent of other students contribute or when they believe that 64 per cent of other students contribute? Panel II shows the probit model with the reported beliefs incorporated as an independent variable. A change in expectation from 46 per cent to 64 per cent would reflect a change in the contribution probability of around 11.5 percentage points.[6] This effect is more than double the behavioural change that actually occurs due to conditional cooperation. The correlation between elicited expectations and behaviour therefore greatly overestimates the effect of conditional cooperation. This can be explained by a 'false consensus' effect: one's own behaviour influences the expectations about others to a certain extent. The 'type' of person therefore not only influences the pro-social behaviour but also the expectation about the pro-social behaviour of others. Panel III of Table 4.3 controls for the 'type' of person by incorporating the coefficient of past behaviour into the probit model. In this specification, the marginal effect of a one-percentage change in expectations is 0.003 at the mean value. A change in expectations from 46 per cent to 64 per cent would correspond to a change in the contribution probability of around 5.3 percentage points. This effect is more in line with the behavioural change resulting from induced beliefs, because the coefficient of past behaviour captures part of the 'false consensus' effect.

In order to illustrate who reacts the most sensitively to the behaviour of others, Figure 4.3 shows the behavioural differences between individuals in treatment group 'High' versus those in 'Low', dependent on past behaviour. For example, for those who contributed in half of their previous decision situations ($c = 0.5$), the figure reflects whether people in treatment group 'High' are more likely to contribute than those in treatment 'Low'. The figure confirms the expectation that subjects who never ($c = 0$) or always ($c = 1$) contributed are not very sensitive to the behaviour of others in the particular decision setting. In contrast, subjects who changed their behaviour in the past pay more attention to others' behaviour, according to the theory of conditional cooperation. In particular, those who have contributed less than half of the time but at least once ($0 < c < 0.5$) behave in a way that is especially conditional on the behaviour of others.

The more that people have contributed in the past, the less sensitivity they tend to have to the behaviour of others. People with a strong preference for contributing to the social funds do not seem to care that much about the pro-social behaviour of others, even when they know that the majority are free-riding.[7] This result may be due to the censored decision setting. People who already give the full amount to the funds are not able to increase their contributions further when confronted with the information that many others contribute. The result is consistent with a model where people have heterogeneous preferences. As the decision is censored, people who have strong (or weak) pro-social preferences are not able to further increase (or decrease) their contribution. People who are more indifferent to contributing or not contributing reacted the most strongly to the information about cooperation rates in the field experiment.

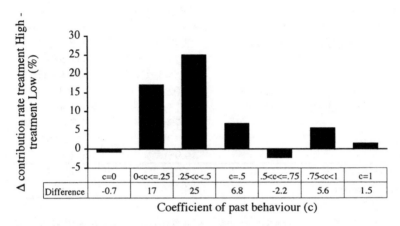

Source: Field experiment, University of Zurich, winter term 2002/3.

Figure 4.3   Different reactions to the behaviour of others

The finding that the treatment effect declines the more that individuals contributed in the past is supported by a probit model. Panel I in Table 4.4 shows the relevant model with an interaction term *Treatment 'High'*Coefficient of past behaviour*. The effect of the treatment declines with the coefficient of past behaviour, as already shown in Figure 4.3. The joint hypothesis of Treatment *'High'* and the interaction effect not being zero is statistically significant at the 90 per cent level ($\chi^2 = 4.87$; $p < 0.088$). However, if the subjects who never contributed in the past are excluded, the relationship becomes much clearer as is shown in Panel II in Table 4.4. In particular, the coefficient of the interaction term *Treatment 'High'* Coefficient of past behaviour* shows that the more individuals contributed in the past, the less they will react to the behaviour of others. The joint hypothesis of Treatment *'High'* and the interaction effect not being zero is statistically significant at the 95 per cent level ($\chi^2 = 8.68$; $p < 0.013$).

Table 4.4   Different reactions to the behaviour of others

Dichotomous dependent variable: Contribution to at least one fund (=1)

Variable	Panel I	Panel II (excluding subjects who never contributed)
Treatment 'High' (64%)	0.198	0.533*
	(1.23)	(2.27)
	[5.0%]	[10.7%]
Treatment 'Low' (46%)	Reference group	
Coefficient of past behaviour	2.735**	3.193**
	(17.27)	(13.89)
	[69.5%]	[63.6%]
Interaction Treatment 'High' *	-0.028	-0.424
Coefficient of past behaviour	(-0.13)	(-1.39)
	[-0.7%]	[-8.4%]
Constant	-1.171**	-1.558**
	(-9.95)	(-8.55)
Number of observations	1,754	1,575
Log Likelihood	-594.276	-504.530

Notes: Coefficients of probit regressions. z-value in parentheses. Marginal effects in brackets. *Level of significance*: * $0.01 < p < 0.05$, ** $p < 0.01$.

Source: Field experiment, University of Zurich, winter term 2002/03.

4.1.1   Framing Effects

Two additional treatments were undertaken in the field experiment in order to investigate whether the framing of the information about the behaviour of others influences pro-social behaviour. The information about average student contributions was therefore also framed *negatively*. In addition to the 2,000 students who were in the two basic treatments, 1,000 students received the information that a low percentage (36 per cent) *did not* contribute (Treatment 'High negative'), and 1,000 students received the information that a high percentage of the student population (54 per cent) *did not* contribute (Treatment 'Low negative'), respectively.

The question thus posed is whether the framing on cooperators or free-riders changes pro-social behaviour. One possible expectation would be that the more one shifts the focal point to the people who do not contribute, the lower the contribution rate would be. The results from the experiment, however, do not support this hypothesis. Table 4.5 presents a conditional logit model which includes individual fixed effects and time dummies and controls for the four main treatment groups.

Table 4.5   Framing effects and conditional cooperation

Dependent variable: Contribution to at least one fund (=1)

Variable	Coefficient	z-value
Treatment 'High' (64%)	0.401**	(3.00)
Treatment 'High negative' (36% not)	0.406**	(3.23)
Treatment 'Low' (46%)	-0.025	(-0.19)
Treatment 'Low negative' (54% not)	0.249	(1.91)
Individual fixed effects	included	
Semester dummies	included	
Number of observations	71,359	
Log likelihood	-26,862.874	

Notes: Conditional logit model with individual fixed effects.
Level of significance: * $0.01 < p < 0.05$, ** $p < 0.01$.

Source: Field experiment, University of Zurich, winter term 2002/03.

Two main results can be seen in Table 4.5:

1. *No statistically significant framing effects can be identified.* People's behaviour does not differ whether they are either in treatment 'High' or in treatment 'High negative'. A χ^2-test for the differences of the coefficient shows that the willingness to contribute increases similarly in both treatments ($\chi^2(1) = 0.00$, $p < 0.978$). The behavioural difference between people who were confronted with either the positively or the negatively framed information that only a *few* contribute to the two funds is also not statistically significant ($\chi^2(1) = 2.30$, $p < 0.129$).

2. *Results concerning conditional cooperation become smaller if the information is framed negatively.* According to the theory of conditional cooperation, a difference between treatments 'High'/'High negative' and between treatments 'Low'/'Low negative' should be expected. In line with conditional cooperation, both treatments 'High' and 'High negative' increase contribution rates, while people's change in behaviour in treatment 'Low' and 'Low negative' is not statistically significant. In detail, while the behaviour in treatment 'Low' is significantly different from the behaviour in both treatment 'High' and treatment 'High negative', behaviour in treatment 'Low negative' does not statistically significantly differ from the behaviour in both treatments with high contribution rates.[8] Informing people about the number of contributors or non-contributors seems not to influence people's conditional

cooperation. Although the effect become smaller, people still increase their contributions if informed about many (few) other contributors (other non-contributors).

The information is as yet insufficient for understanding how framing a situation of few contributors as a situation where many do *not* contribute influences people's behaviour. Interestingly enough, other studies fail to find consistent results for conditional cooperation when decisions are framed differently. Fleishman (1988) finds in his laboratory experiment that a social dilemma framed as taking from a collective good leads people to conform to others' behaviour, whereas framing it as giving to a public good leads people to act even contrary to others' behaviour. Although the framing in this experiment is different to the framing in the field experiment, framing effects and 'conditional cooperation' have to be further investigated and should potentially be explicitly included in models of choice behaviour in public good situations.

4.4   CONCLUSION

This chapter has presented evidence of conditional cooperation in a large-scale field experiment, asking whether people's pro-social behaviour is conditional on the pro-social behaviour of others. When students were presented with the information that many others donated to two social funds at the University of Zurich, their willingness to contribute was higher than that of students who were informed that only a few others contributed. This constitutes the first tests of conditional cooperation in a field experiment about charitable giving.

The result that people's contribution varies positively with the group average has to be refined. Subjects who have never or always contributed in the past are quite insensitive to the treatments. By contrast, subjects who have changed their behaviour in the past pay more attention to others' behaviour. The higher sensitivity is consistent with a model where people have heterogeneous preferences. As the decision is censored, people who have strong (or weak) pro-social preferences are not able to further increase (or decrease) their contribution. People who are more indifferent about contributing or not contributing react *ceteris paribus* most significantly to the information about cooperation rates.

The results of the field experiment on conditional cooperation are highly relevant to theories of pro-social behaviour and have important policy implications. In the following I sketch the implications of conditional cooperation for economic theory and policy:

1. *Theory* The behaviour resulting from conditional cooperation is consistent with at least three theoretical hypotheses: firstly, people want to behave in an appropriate way and conform to a social norm (for example, Messick, 1999); secondly, people have some sort of fairness preferences such as reciprocity (for example, Fehr and Gächter, 2000b); or thirdly, contributions by others serve as a signal for the quality of the public good, or for the organization which provides the good (for example, a charity) (for example, Vesterlund, 2003). The results of the field experiment do not clarify which theoretical approach is the most appropriate for explaining conditional cooperation. Results of previous experiments that attempt to discriminate between the various explanations are ambiguous. Some experimental studies indicate that conformity can explain conditional cooperation better than reciprocal considerations (for example, Bohnet and Zeckhauser, 2002), while others come to the opposite conclusion (Falk et al., 2003; Kurzban et al., 2001). Yet other laboratory experiments find evidence for the third hypothesis that the cooperative behaviour of others is used as a signal for the quality of the public good (Potters et al., 2005). To proceed, future research should concentrate on testing in the fields the conditions under which particular motives lead to conditional cooperation. The motives for behaviour conditioned by the acts of others probably depend as much on the decision situation as do the motivations to behave pro-socially in the first place. In situations where altruism is the most prominent motive for behaving pro-socially, as in charitable giving, the signalling and conformity explanations may be more important, whereas in smaller-group contributions to public goods, for example, not overusing a common property resource, it is reciprocal considerations that may lead to conditional behaviour.

2. *Policy implications* Almost all models of social comparison and pro-social behaviour have multiple equilibria: a 'good' equilibrium where all people contribute and a 'bad' equilibrium where nobody contributes to the public good. To derive policy implications, the question has to be answered about how best to coordinate the 'good' equilibrium. A number of authors propose that, because expectations about the behaviour of others are crucial if multiple equilibria exist, *belief management* should bring about a cascade towards almost full contribution and pro-social behaviour (see, for example, Kahan, 2002). Beliefs about the behaviour of others can thus be manipulated if the visibility of anti-social behaviour, such as littering or criminal activities, can be suppressed by selectively informing the public or by removing the signs of the anti-social behaviour (for example, litter), as fast as possible.[9] A second possibility for exploiting the tendency towards

conditional cooperation would be to introduce the composition of neighborhoods as a factor. Moving low-income families into richer neighborhoods would, for example, decrease the likelihood of children from the low-income families committing crime (Ludwig et al., 2001; Moffitt, 2001). A third possibility for achieving the 'good' equilibrium would be to rely on the law as a coordination device. People could then take the behavioural rules set by law as a signal for appropriate behaviour. The results of the experiments by Bohnet and Cooter (2003) show that more research has to be undertaken to establish whether the law really can lead to a 'good' equilibrium in other than coordination games, that is in public good situations. According to their results, this has to be doubted.

The proposals neglect, however, to consider the incentives of politicians. Politicians have, for example, very low incentives to put poor families into rich neighbourhoods because wealthy voters might oppose policies which appear to decrease the 'quality' of the neighbourhood and hence result in lower values of their houses. In addition, belief management might be used by politicians very selectively because beliefs about pro-social behaviour also influence the probability of re-election. The important consideration that the performance of politicians may be biased is at odds with the idea of political competition. To assess the expected effect of various policy implications, it is therefore crucially important to take the incentives of politicians into account.

Both economic theory and policy has to take into account the result that people's behaviour is conditional on the behaviour of the group average. If such behavioural regularity is incorporated, behavioural predictions will become more accurate and policy-makers can take full advantage of the fact that a small change in policy can have tremendous effects on the equilibrium.

NOTES

1. For a collection of problems in identifying social interaction effects, see Manski (1993, 2000) and Glaeser and Scheinkman (2001).
2. Subjects of the field experiment on matching donations (see Chapter 5) are also excluded from the control group. The results are, however, not sensitive to the inclusion of these subjects.
3. The different time periods were indicated on the information sheets by stating that either '…% of the students contributed in the last semester' or '… in the last semesters'.
4. Glaeser et al. (2000: 833) found evidence of such an effect in their study of trust. They conclude: '…the best way to determine whether or not a person is trustworthy is to ask him whether or not he trusts others.' However, Fehr et al. (2002), in their large-scale combination of survey methods with experiments, cannot reproduce these results. In their

study, 'none of the survey measures of trust are good predictors of trustworthiness in the experiment' (p. 12).

5.   Ashraf, et al. (2002) use dictator game giving by individuals to explain behaviour in trust games. Similar to the approach used here, they use revealed behaviour to undertake a within-subject analysis.

6.   I calculated the difference between the contribution probabilities at the two points of interest on the cumulative standard normal function: $\Phi(\text{constant term} + 64^*\beta_{\text{expectation}})$ - $\Phi(\text{constant term} + 46^*\beta_{\text{expectation}})$. If there are other variables in the equation, they are included at their mean value.

7.   This result can be compared to results of a field experiment by Falk and Ichino (2003). They show that an experimentally manipulated high productivity norm increases the productivity of the least productive subject, but a low productivity norm does not have much influence on the most productive subjects.

8.   The χ^2-tests for the differences of the coefficient show the following results: difference between treatment 'High negative'-treatment 'Low': $\chi2(1) = 5.93$, $p < 0.0148$; difference between treatment 'High'-treatment 'Low negative': $\chi2(1) = 0.70$, $p < 0.4025$; difference between Treatment 'High negative'-'Low negative': $\chi2(1) = 0.80$, $p < 0.3723$.

9.   In the private sector, fundraisers exploit people's tendency to mimic others' behaviour by announcing what the others have given. They list leaders' donations or establish 'seed money' before asking further potential donors (see Andreoni and Petrie, 2004).

APPENDIX

Informationsblatt

Wir möchten Ihnen dieses Semester Informationen zu den freiwilligen Beiträgen für die beiden Fonds ‚Stiftung Darlehenskasse der Studentenschaft' (CHF 7.-) und ‚Solidaritätsfonds für ausländische Studierende' (CHF 5.-) zukommen lassen:

64 % aller Studierenden zahlten im letzten Semester in die beiden Fonds ein.

Figure 4.A.1   Sample information sheet of field experiment

Table 4.A.1   Contributions to both funds and others' behaviour

Dichotomous dependent variable: Contribution to both funds (= 1)

Variable	Coefficient	z-value	$p > |z|$
Treatment 'High' (64%)	0.397**	(3.21)	0.001
Treatment 'Low' (46%)	0.11	(0.90)	0.370
Individual fixed effects	included		
Semester dummies	included		
Number of observations	78,232		
Log likelihood	-29,550.178		

Notes: Test of differences for treatment 'High' - 'Low' = 0.0: $\chi^2(1) = 2.82$, $p < 0.0932$. Conditional logit model with individual fixed effects. z-values in parentheses. *Level of significance*: * $0.01 < p < 0.05$, ** $p < 0.01$.

Source: Field experiment, University of Zurich, winter term 2002/03.

5. Matching Donations: Subsidizing Pro-social Behaviour

Donations to charitable organizations and contributions to public goods are important activities for society. Many charitable organizations depend fully on private contributions. The question on how giving behaviour can be actively fostered is therefore important for these organizations and for the private provision of public goods in general. From the point of view of economic theory, decreasing the price of a donated monetary unit should stimulate donations. Such subsidizing can be done either by a rebate or a matching mechanism that supports charitable giving. Concerning the rebate mechanism, there is substantial literature on how tax deductions for charitable contributions influence their size. For an overview of the results, see Chapter 2.

A second approach to subsidizing charitable contributions is to match donations. A matching donations' mechanism decreases the cost of giving because the donors' contribution is worth more. This mechanism is popular in a number of corporations in the USA and in Europe, where employers match charitable contributions on the part of their employees. There is, however, little research that analyses the effect of matching donations on charitable contributions. One reason for this may be the statistical problem involved. If one were to observe that employees of a firm with a matching mechanism donate more than the employees of a firm without such a mechanism, this would not support the hypothesis that matching leads to a behavioural effect. The higher contribution rate in the first firm may be due to various reasons not connected with the matching mechanism; for instance, it may be that, due to the fact that the first firm has a matching mechanism, more pro-social employees select to work for that firm. To test the effect of matching donations, people have to be randomly assigned to a matching mechanism. This can be analysed in an experimental setting. Eckel and Grossman (2003) present the first study I am aware of which systematically analyses matching donations in a laboratory experiment (for a replication and a critic of the results, see Davis et al., 2005; for a field experiment, see Eckel and Grossman, 2005). They analyse whether the rebate scheme and the matching mechanism lead to the same behavioural effects. From a theoretical point of view the two mechanisms should yield the same results. It should not matter whether you pay 50 cents for a $1 donation due to the fact that you get 50 cents back or someone increases your donation by 50 cents. The results of the experiments show, however, that it is important whether the rebate mechanism or the matching mechanism is used. Matching donations leads to a higher amount of charitable giving than a rebate and is therefore more effective.

This chapter tests the effect of matching donations in a *controlled field experiment*. The donations of two groups of 300 students each are matched by 25 per cent and by 50 per cent respectively if they contribute to *both* funds. The resulting behaviour is compared with the control group, whose donations are not matched. The results of the field experiment support the hypothesis that matching donations increase the contributions to a public good. However, the effect depends first of all on the amount paid on top. Firstly, while the lower amount has no statistically significant effect on the willingness to contribute, the higher amount does affect the likelihood of contributing. Secondly, the effect of matching donations depends on the 'type' of person whose potential donations are subsidized. People need to be already pro-socially inclined to react to the relative price effect of the matching mechanism.

The effect of the donation-matching mechanism is not trivial due to two possible counterproductive effects. Firstly, a classical crowding-out effect can decrease the overall amount donated so that people reduce their contribution to the point that the total amount of giving (the matched contributions included) equals the amount donated without matching. Secondly, a motivational crowding-out effect can take place (Deci and Ryan, 1980, 1985; Frey, 1997). People may perceive the donation matching as controlling, which may destroy their intrinsic motivation to donate. When the matching amount is very small, a motivational crowding-out effect may be stronger than the ordinary price effect and donations may decline. The result of the field experiment can neither confirm nor deny the two counterproductive effects. However, some patterns of behavioural reaction to the donation-matching mechanism suggest that there is more at work than just the normal relative price effect.

5.1   DESIGN OF FIELD EXPERIMENT

In the experimental intervention, two groups of 300 students were each selected randomly and provided with information about the matching mechanism. With the official letter for renewing the registration and the decision about contributing to the two funds (for the winter semester 2002/03), the University administration supplied the selected students with a sheet of paper containing the following information: 'If you contribute to *both* social funds, an anonymous donor will match your contribution by CHF 3' (treatment 'Matching 25%'), or 'CHF 6' (treatment 'Matching 50%'). The potential donations are therefore matched by 25 per cent and 50 per cent, respectively. The sheet of paper that the two treatment groups received differed only with respect to the amount matched. The subjects were informed that the matched money would be split equally between the two funds. The two funds received the additional money after the experiment.

Due to the 'institutional difference' that freshmen have to pick up the registration form at the counter of the administration office, only students who had registered and decided at least once in the past are in the treatment groups. The freshmen are also excluded from the control group. Students who were part of any other treatment, that is the field experiment discussed in Chapter 4, were also excluded from the control group. As most treatments were designed to increase the donations (which was a precondition for the University administration's participation), subjects of other treatments would have biased the behaviour of the control group. As some of the students decided not to renew their registration, the decisions of 532 subjects in the two treatment groups could be observed. Students decide anonymously at home about the contribution to the two social funds.

Table 5.1 shows the summary statistics for the control group and the treatment group. As the assignment was random, no significant differences emerged between the characteristics of subjects in the treatment group and the rest of the student population.

Table 5.1   Summary statistics for donations, winter term 2002/03

Personal characteristics	Control group	Treatment 'M 25%'	Treatment 'M 50%'
Number of observations	12,518	265	267
Number of semesters	11.5 (8.3)	11.3 (8.3)	11.3 (7.4)
Age	28.3 (7.3)	28.5 (7.7)	28.0 (7.8)
Gender (female = 1)	51%	53%	50%
Economists (= 1)	11%	9%	12%
Coefficient of past behaviour	0.73 (0.36)	0.71 (0.38)	0.73 (0.35)

Notes: Standard deviations in parentheses

Source: Field experiment, University of Zurich, winter term 2002/03.

The data set has some special characteristics which may be important, especially when comparing the results of the analysis to results from laboratory experiments. Firstly, the field experiment is based on a trichotomous decision. Students can decide whether to contribute to no fund, one fund or both funds. Most students decide either not to contribute at all or to contribute to both funds. No marginal adjustment is possible in the sense that people increase their contribution by one or more monetary units. This means that students are censored in their decision because they cannot increase or decrease their contributions if they already give the full amount or nothing. The expected effect of a change in relative prices should therefore be small. Secondly, people in the treatment group have decided whether to contribute or not at least once before the field experiment started. On average, subjects had decided 10 times previous to the start of the experiment. If contributing has become a habit, the donation matching must be expected to have limited effects on behaviour.

The next section presents the hypotheses for the field experiment.

5.2   BEHAVIOURAL HYPOTHESES

Charitable giving is subject to the relative price effect, just like any other activity: if donations are getting cheaper, people will undertake this activity more. For the field experiment, this leads to three hypotheses:

HYPOTHESIS 1: More people will donate to both funds in the treatment groups than in the control group, because matching makes giving cheaper than in the treatment groups.

HYPOTHESIS 2: The higher the matching benefit of each Swiss franc donated, the more people will donate. In the field experiment, more people are expected to donate in treatment 'Matching 50%' than in the treatment 'Matching 25%'.

HYPOTHESIS 3: People who otherwise donate to only one of the funds will be strongly motivated to contribute to both funds due to the fact that they can 'profit' from the whole matching amount by a slight increase in their contribution.

The derived hypotheses are based on assumptions about (1) the character of the charitable giving and (2) the effect of a change in relative prices. However, these assumptions are crucial, because there are counterproductive effects which can put the hypothesis in question.

1.   Charitable donations are assumed to have a joy-of-giving (or 'warm glow') effect (for example, Andreoni, 1990; Cornes and Sandler, 1994). This suggests that it is important that people personally donate to the two funds. The larger the effect they can personally achieve by donating, the more they will enjoy giving. This assumption contrasts with the neutrality results of public goods models, where people reduce their

donations when they see that the government or other individuals increase their share of the public good (Roberts, 1984; Andreoni, 1988). Pure altruism models predict that the donation-matching mechanism would influence people to decrease their share, because, due to the matched amount, they can produce the same donation amount as if no such mechanism existed. Which model is appropriate is an empirical issue. Pure altruism models are not supported in the empirical literature: people's donations are not completely crowded-out by government contributions (see Chapter 2), nor do people reduce their contribution when the contributions of others increase, as was seen in Chapter 4.

2. A motivational crowding-out effect can work against the relative price effect (Frey, 1997a). People who donate in an anonymous situation to a public good have an intrinsic motivation to do so. Due to the underlying incentive structure, contributions are not utility-maximizing in strictly monetary terms. Offering these individuals a matching mechanism can be perceived as controlling. According to Deci (1975) and Deci and Ryan (1985), this may lead to a decrease in pro-social behaviour, due to a perceived reduction in self-determination. A quite different explanation for a detrimental effect of monetary incentives may be based on the prestige motive of charitable giving. A monetary incentive to behave pro-socially may decrease the value of the generosity being signalled. If people are motivated to contribute to a charity in order to signal to themselves ('warm glow') or to others that they are generous, monetary incentives can decrease this signal because it will become more and more unclear whether people are behaving pro-socially out of generosity or because of the monetary incentives. According to this reasoning, a possible empirical test would analyse whether charitable donations make people less happy when the tax incentives for donations are increased.

A strong motivational crowding-out effect may lead to an overall effect that works contrary to the relative price effect (see Chapter 2 for an overview). There can be two diverging overall effects of matching contributions. Firstly, the crowding-out effect may dominate the relative price effect of matching. This is likely to be the case when the relative price effect is small, as in the small matching treatment ('Matching 25'). Secondly, the relative price effect may dominate the crowding-out effect. This is likely to be the case when the incentives based on matching are large ('Matching 50'). Gneezy (2003) and Gneezy and Rusticini (2000) find experimental support for the proposition that the relative price effect dominates when the monetary reward is sufficiently large. If, however, the incentive, that is the matching mechanism, is perceived as supportive, intrinsic motivation may even be strengthened. An external intervention would then crowd in pro-social behaviour.

In addition to the two counterproductive effects, people may be heterogeneous in their pro-social preferences, which might be important with respect to the effect of matching donations. As stated in a survey on previous experimental studies, 'the most important heterogeneity is the one between purely selfish subjects and fair-minded subjects' (Fehr and Schmidt, 2003: 247). Pure egoists, who are not pro-socially inclined towards the funds at all, are not expected to react to the relative price effect induced by the donation-matching mechanism. In the following section, these hypotheses are tested.

5.3   ANALYSIS AND RESULTS

5.3.1   Effect of Matching Donations

Table 5.2 presents the descriptive statistics for the field experiments. The table shows the contribution rates to both funds; only one fund or no fund for the control group and the two treatment groups in the semester when the field experiment was undertaken. The three columns in the lower part of the table present Mann-Whitney tests for the differences in contribution rates between the control and the treatment groups, and between the two treatment groups.

Table 5.2 shows two results, which are only partly in line with the hypotheses:

1.   People react to the matching donations' mechanism. If the two treatment groups are taken together, contribution rates to both funds are higher in the treatment groups than in the control group. These figures are consistent with Hypothesis 1, suggesting that people react to the relative price effect. However, no statistically significant difference between control and treatment group emerges. The increasing effect of matching donations is only present for the treatment 'Matching 50%'. As revealed in Table 5.2, the contribution rate to both funds is 3.67 percentage points higher than in the control group ($p < 0.210$). In line with Hypothesis 1, the effect is bigger for a higher matching donation. But for treatment 'Matching 25%', the contribution rate to both funds is even lower than for the control group. These differences are not statistically significant.

2.   The patterns of giving to only one fund or no fund are consistent with Hypothesis 2. Individuals stop contributing to only one fund, because with just a slightly higher contribution, subjects can 'gain' the whole matching amount. This applies especially for the higher incentive to contribute, when the contribution rate to only one fund is 3.10 percentage points lower for treatment 'Matching 50%' compared to the control group. This effect is statistically significant at the 95 per cent

level. The contribution rate to only one fund is also lower for treatment 'Matching 25%', but the difference is not statistically significant. Interestingly enough, a larger number of subjects do not contribute at all in treatment 'Matching 25%', compared to the control group. For the treatment 'Matching 50%', the contribution rates are as expected. The percentage of people who do not contribute at all decreases. The descriptive analysis shows that the effect of matching donations comes from the high matching mechanism, and mostly from subjects who change from giving to one fund to giving to both funds. The effect of the matching mechanism to start giving at all seems quite modest.

Table 5.2   Patterns of giving to the two funds across treatments

Contribution to ...	Control group	Treatment 'M 25%'	Treatment 'M 50%'
... both funds	66.37%	65.66%	70.04%
	(0.45)	(2.9)	(2.8)
... only one fund	6.47%	4.91%	3.37%
	(0.24)	(1.3)	(1.1)
... neither of the funds	27.16%	29.43%	26.59%
	(0.43)	(2.80)	(2.70)

	Difference 'M 25%'-Control	Difference 'M 50%'-Control	Difference 'M 50'-'M 25'
... both funds	-0.71%	3.67%	4.38%
	($z = 0.241$;	($z = 1.254$;	($z = 1.080$:
	$p < 0.810$)	$p < 0.210$)	$p < 0.280$)
... only one fund	-1.57%	-3.10%	-1.53%
	($z = 1.027$;	($z = 2.046$;	($z = 0.888$;
	$p < 0.305$)	$p < 0.041$)	$p < 0.374$)
... neither of the funds	2.27%	-0.57%	-2.84%
	($z = 0.822$;	($z = 0.206$;	($z = 0.729$;
	$p < 0.411$)	$p < 0.837$)	$p < 0.466$)

Notes: Standard errors in parentheses. Mann-Whitney test for significance of differences.

Source: Field experiment, University of Zurich, winter term 2002/03.

In the above analysis, individual heterogeneity generates a lot of interference, which makes it difficult to estimate the effect of matching donations. A logit model was therefore estimated taking into account individual fixed effects and semester dummies. Although the subjects are randomly assigned to the different treatment groups, the fixed-effects model allows reducing the noise in the estimations.

Table 5.3 presents the results for the logit model with individual fixed effects. The dependent variable takes the value 1 if people contribute to both funds and 0 otherwise. The general picture of Table 5.2 is confirmed. The probability that subjects faced with the mechanism 'Matching 50%' will contribute to both funds increases in a statistically significant way (at the 90 per cent level). The effect of 'Matching 25%' on the contribution rate of subjects in this treatment group is half as large. The behavioural difference, compared to the control group, is not statistically significant. The results are consistent with hypothesis 1 and hypothesis 2 in so far as the amount of matching is decisive for the success of the donation-matching mechanisms. The results suggest that a small change in relative prices does not produce any significant effect on behaviour.

Table 5.3   Effect of matching donations

Dichotomous dependent variable: Contribution to both funds (=1)

Variable	Coefficient	z-value	$p > |z|$
Treatment 'Matching 25%'	0.278	(1.29)	0.195
Treatment 'Matching 50%'	0.469*	(2.15)	0.032
Individual fixed effects	included		
Semester dummies	included		
Number of observations	75,741		
Log likelihood	-28,617.166		

Notes: Conditional logit model with individual fixed effects. Test of differences for treatment 'Matching 25%' - 'Matching 50%' = 0.0: $\chi^2(1) = 0.39, p < 0.5309$.
Level of significance: * $0.01 < p < 0.05$, ** $p < 0.01$.

Source: Field experiment, University of Zurich, winter term 2002/03.

Although the results are not as strong as in Eckel and Grossman (2003), they do show that a matching mechanism has a positive effect on pro-social behaviour in a field setting. Depending on the underlying motives for contributing to the two funds, the positive effect of the matching mechanism can be due to various reasons. Firstly, the matching mechanism can trigger a relative price effect, where an individual's contribution has a larger effect with the same monetary outlay. Secondly, the fact that an anonymous donor is matching the contributions of the students may be interpreted as a positive signal for the quality of the social funds. People may, therefore, be more inclined to contribute. Thirdly, the fact that somebody else is socially concerned and matches the contributions of the students may be seen as a nice act, which a conditional cooperator may want to reciprocate. As the analysis in its present form is not able to discriminate between these explanations, further studies should try to distinguish between these channels of a matching mechanism. The results should then be compared to the effects on charitable giving of mechanisms similar to matching donations, for example 'seed money' (List and Lucking-Reiley, 2002; List and Rondeau, 2003) and 'leadership giving' (for example, Vesterlund, 2003).

In order to come to a better understanding of how the matching mechanism influences giving behaviour, the next section analyses who in fact is most sensitive to the change in the price of giving induced by the donation-matching mechanism.

5.3.2   Who Reacts to Matching Donations?

People are heterogeneous with respect to their pro-social preferences. Some may be selfishly inclined, while others place more emphasis on other people's well-being (or have pro-social preferences for other reasons). In this section, the giving patterns of various 'types' of people and their reaction to a change in the price of giving is analysed.

In the panel data set, past behaviour is used as a proxy for the subjects' pro-social inclination. The coefficient of past behaviour indicates the fraction of previous occasions on which the subject decided to contribute to at least one of the two funds (see Chapter 4 for a detailed description). People who never contributed to even one fund are not expected to react to matching donations. People who always contributed in the past are also not expected to react much to the change in relative prices because their decision is censored. Even if they wanted to increase their contribution due to the higher effectiveness of their donation, they are not able to give more money to the two funds. The effect of matching donations is therefore underestimated.

Figure 5.1 shows the effect of the treatment 'Matching 50%' on the different types compared to the control group. The figure shows, for example, whether people who contributed in half of their decisions to at least one fund ($c = 0.5$) are more likely than the control group to contribute when they are in the treatment 'Matching 50%' (for the contribution rates of both treatments, see Figure 5.A.1 in the Appendix).

The figure is consistent with the hypothesis that selfish people do not react positively to matched donations. Matching is a policy instrument which does not seem to be able to activate pro-social behaviour in selfishly inclined persons. This result is in line with empirical studies that analyse the effect of taxes on charitable giving. Clotfelter (1980) presents evidence that new itemizers may be less sensitive to price changes than former itemizers. Even if the price of giving decreases, donating is still an altruistic act and selfish types will not be convinced to start donating. Figure 5.1 shows that, for people who have never contributed in the past, the donation-matching mechanism even has a strong negative effect.[1] The mechanism may strengthen their conviction not to contribute. In terms of evaluating the roots of the detrimental effect of monetary incentives, this result is informative because it is not consistent with the suggestion that intrinsic motivation to behave pro-socially can be crowded out. People who have never contributed in the past can be assumed to have little intrinsic motivation. Nevertheless, the incentives given by the matching mechanism seem to allow selfish students to further legitimize their selfish behaviour. The various mechanisms leading to the negative effects of monetary incentives are far from being completely understood.

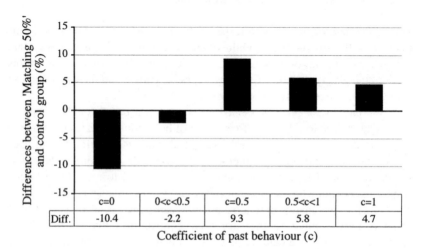

Source: Field experiment, University of Zurich, winter term 2002/03.

Figure 5.1   Different reactions to matching donations

In contrast, the effect of matching donations has the greatest positive effect on pro-socially inclined people. People who have contributed half of the time to at least one fund react the most. For people who almost always contributed in the past, this means that they do not stop contributing.[2] The donation-matching mechanism therefore helps to stabilize the contributions of the most pro-socially inclined subjects. One has to be aware that the students are censored in their decisions. For example, people who always donated to the two funds may be prepared to increase their donations even more in the matching scheme. It is therefore possible that the stronger the preference to contribute to the two funds as indicated by the coefficient of past behaviour, the more sensitive people are to the price of giving.

Table 5.4   Pro-socially inclined people react to matching donations

Dichotomous dependent variable: Contribution to both funds (=1)

Variable	Panel I			Panel II		
Treatment 'M 25%'	-0.00	(-0.00)	[0.0]	0.128	(1.38)	[4.2]
Treatment 'M 50%'	0.136(*)	(1.66)	[4.9]	0.187*	(2.07)	[6.0]
Gender (Female = 1)	-0.081**	(-3.51)	[-3.0]	-0.098**	(-3.92)	[-3.3]
Economists (=1)	-0.184**	(-4.99)	[-7.0]	-0.204**	(-5.12)	[-7.2]
Age	0.018**	(8.03)	[0.7]	0.017**	(6.99)	[0.6]
Number of semesters	-0.022**	(-11.32)	[-0.8]	-0.018**	(-8.58)	[-0.6]
Constant	0.196**	(3.67)		0.355**	(6.18)	
Number of observations	13,050			11,718		
Log likelihood	-8,337.85			-6,974.16		

Notes: Coefficients of probit regressions. *z*-values in parentheses. Marginal effects in brackets. Panel II excludes people who never contributed in the past.
Level of significance: (*) $0.05 < p < 0.1$, * $0.01 < p < 0.05$, ** $p < 0.01$.

Source: Field experiment, University of Zurich, winter term 2002/03.

Table 5.4 presents a probit model for the semester in which the field experiment was undertaken. The dependent variable is 1 when people contributed to both funds in the semester under analysis. As the coefficients in the probit model are difficult to interpret, marginal effects are computed, indicating how much the probability of contribution changes compared to the reference group. Panel I covers all subjects in order to test the effect of being in the two treatments. Control variables are gender (female = 1), being an economist (=1), age and number of semesters. The results show that the treatment 'Matching 50%' increases the probability of contribution to the two funds by 4.9 percentage points. This effect is statistically significant at the 90 per cent level. The treatment 'Matching 25%' has no effect on the probability of contributing to both funds. However, these results look different when one *excludes* subjects who have never contributed in the past. Panel II shows the result for this subsample. The marginal effect of treatment 'Matching 50%' increases to 6 percentage points ($p < 0.05$), while the marginal effect of treatment 'Matching 25%' increases to 4.2 percentage points, but is not statistically significant. For those people who are pro-socially inclined, both treatments with either lower or larger matching seem to have a positive effect on contributions.

The *control variables* show the following effects: the probability that women will contribute to both funds is 3 percentage points lower than for men. *Gender*, as well as all other control variables, has a coefficient which is statistically significant at a 99 per cent level. The gender effect contradicts other studies, which find that women tend to be more generous in donating (for example, Eckel and Grossman, 1997). However, there are also studies in line with the estimates (for a review, see Eckel and Grossman, 2001). In the next subsection, the gender effect is more closely investigated. *Economists* behave less pro-socially than non-economists. As shown in the next chapter, this is mostly due to a selection effect. *Age* has a positive effect on pro-social behaviour. Older people behave more pro-socially than younger people. This result is in line with many studies about giving behaviour (for a survey, see Clotfelter, 1997). With *repetition of the decision*, people's willingness to contribute to both funds decreases (Ledyard, 1995).

5.3.3   Gender Differences and the Price of Pro-social Behaviour

The results of the empirical analysis suggest that women tend to behave less pro-socially than men. This result has to be seen in the context of a long list of studies investigating which sex behaves more fairly (for a survey, see Croson and Gneezy, 2005). As the results of these studies are diverse, Andreoni and Vesterlund (2001) investigate whether the price of giving may explain differences in the pro-social behaviour between men and women. They show that the demand functions for the pro-social behaviour of men and women intersect. Men behave more pro-socially when prices are low; however, when the cost of undertaking a pro-social act increases, women tend to behave more altruistically than men. This result cannot be found in all experimental studies. Eckel and Grossman (1996b: 144) conclude in their study that 'men's behaviour appears to be unaffected by [the] relative price'.[3]

The field experiment presented in this chapter allows testing in a natural setting whether men and women react differently to price changes for pro-social behaviour. The results do not support the results by Andreoni and Vesterlund. Figure 5.2 shows the contribution rates for men and women to both funds, depending on the different prices of giving in the treatment groups. Women are less willing to contribute to the two funds in the control group (64.4 per cent contribution rate versus 66.2 per cent; t-test of differences: $t = 2.15$; $p < 0.0315$). As the price of giving decreases, women become more willing to contribute to the two funds, while for men the willingness does not increase to the same amount and even decreases for treatment 'Matching 25%'. The demand functions of men and women tend to intersect. The difference, however, is not statistically significant, as revealed by a difference-in-difference analysis (for the results, see Table 5.A.1 in the Appendix). The results suggest that the results by Andreoni and Vesterlund (2001) do not necessarily generalize to field experiments. Further investigation is needed to ascertain whether gender differences emerge in respect to changes in relative prices for pro-social behaviour.

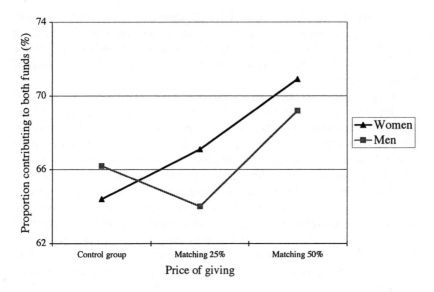

Source: Field experiment, University of Zurich, winter term 2002/03.

Figure 5.2   Gender differences and price of giving

5.4   CONCLUSION

This chapter has tested the effect of a matching mechanism on donations in a controlled field experiment. The donations of students at the University of Zurich were matched. The results support the hypothesis that a matching mechanism increases contributions to a public good in a field setting. However, the effect depends on how much the contributions are matched. Whereas a 25 per cent increase of a donation does not increase the willingness to contribute, a 50 per cent increase does have an effect.

In addition, people need to be socially inclined to react to the matching mechanism. As people have heterogeneous pro-social preferences, they react differently to a change in the price of giving. On the one hand, as in a standard model, people who strongly prefer not to contribute to the two funds are not expected to react to a change in relative prices. By changing the relative prices of giving, selfish types cannot be motivated to behave pro-socially. On the other hand, people who have a strong preference for pro-social behaviour will react the most. As the decision to contribute to the two funds is censored, people who always gave the maximum amount to the two funds cannot increase their contribution more. On the one hand, it makes perfect sense that people who did not contribute in all their previous decisions would have the biggest increase in contributions. On the other hand, the general effect of a matching mechanism may be underestimated due to the fact that pro-socially inclined people would increase their donations if they had the opportunity.

The question remains whether the results of the field experiment can provide information about a potential motivational crowding effect of the matching mechanism. Some results are consistent with a crowding effect of monetary incentives. For example, if the donations are matched by a relatively small amount, the share of students who do not contribute to any fund increases. However, the effects are not large and not statistically significant. Interestingly enough, matching the contributions of people who never contributed in the past slightly decreases their willingness to contribute. Neither result, however, is conclusive enough to answer whether one should expect a detrimental effect from matching donations or what mechanisms would lead to such a crowding-out of pro-social behaviour. It is therefore important to study further the effect of monetary incentives on pro-social behaviour.

NOTES

1.   A negative effect may be possible, because some people who have never contributed in the past may start contributing. However, the probability that this will happen decreases for people in the treatment group.
2.   The willingness to contribute to the funds otherwise decreases with repetition (see Chapter 3).
3.   For a field study on the generosity of men and women, see Andreoni et al. (2003). In their analysis of the charitable giving of married couples and single men and women, they find significant differences between the generosity of men and women depending on the price of giving. Their analysis, however, is more focused on the bargaining process about charitable giving in the household than on the differences in pro-social behaviour of men and women, which may explain the different results of laboratory experiments.

APPENDIX

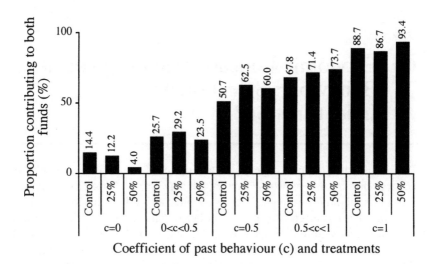

Notes: '25%' refers to treatment 'Matching 25%' while '50%' refers to 'Matching 50%'.

Source: Field experiment, University of Zurich, winter term 2002/3.

Figure 5.A.1   *Contribution rate to both funds depending on treatment and coefficient of past behaviour*

Table 5.A.1   *Gender differences and price of giving*

Dependent variable: Contribution to both funds (=1)

Treatment 'Matching 25%'	-0.059	(-0.51)	[-2.2%]
Treatment 'Matching 50%'	0.083	(0.72)	[3.0%]
Treatment '25%'*Gender	0.135	(0.84)	[4.8%]
Treatment '50%'*Gender	0.099	(0.61)	[3.6%]
Gender (female=1)	-0.049**	(-2.14)	[-1.8%]
Constant	0.418***	(25.23)	
Number of observations	13,058		
Log likelihood	-8,420.2384		

Notes: Coefficient of probit regression. *z*-value in parentheses. Marginal effects in brackets. A test of joint significance of the two interaction terms is not statistically significant on a conventional level; $\chi^2(2) = 1.05$, $p < 0.5911$.
Level of significance: * $0.05 < p < 0.1$, ** $0.01 < p < 0.05$, *** $p < 0.01$.

Source: Field experiment, University of Zurich, winter term 2002/3.

6.   Economic Education and Pro-social Behaviour: Selection or Indoctrination?[*]

Pro-social behaviour may depend not only on social comparisons and relative costs, as discussed in previous chapters, but may also be shaped by education. Education might, for example, influence beliefs about the behaviour of others in a way that has effects for pro-social behaviour. Particularly in situations where multiple equilibria exist, even small changes in beliefs may be crucial for the maintenance of pro-social behaviour. If a certain kind of education therefore systematically lowers the provision of public goods, then such a negative relationship has to be analysed with a view to possibly correcting it.

Economics training is one kind of education which is constantly accused of preventing the provision of public goods by lowering students' pro-social behaviour. Economic science has, according to this claim, a blind spot. It is said that, while students are taught efficiency, equity is not given its due weight in the education of economists. Moreover, it is argued that the *homo oeconomicus* is too narrowly defined, and that it does not explain the behaviour of human beings accurately. A consequence of this oversimplified description of human behaviour is that students of economics act more selfishly than students of other social sciences (for example, Kelman, 1987). Ostrom (1998: 18) explicitly warns: 'We are producing generations of cynical citizens with little trust in one another, much less in their government. Given the central role of trust in solving social dilemmas, we may be creating the very conditions that undermine our own democratic ways of life.' The 'ruthless' behaviour of firms may be partly explained by the economic educations of their chief executive officers's. Daboub et al. (1995: 165), for example, believe that 'corporate illegal activity will be stronger for firms whose TMT's [Top Management Team] have a greater amount of formal management education (i.e., a greater percentage of MBAs)'. According to these views, economists *create* the type of selfish persons (the *homo oeconomicus*) they axiomatically assume in their theories. If this claim holds

* This chapter is based on Meier, Stephan and Bruno S. Frey (2004). Do Business Students Make Good Citizens? *International Journal of the Economics of Business* 11(2). 141-63.

in reality, then critics are right to emphasize that economic science makes much-needed cooperation in the world more difficult.

In this chapter, the claim about the negative influence of economics education on pro-social behaviour will be investigated empirically using the contributions to the two social funds at the University of Zurich. Section 6.1 emphasizes the difference between the analysis undertaken and the empirical approach from previous studies. Section 6.2 presents the two behavioural hypotheses: selection and indoctrination. In Section 6.3 the empirical analysis and the results are discussed. Section 6.4 draws conclusions.

6.1   PREVIOUS RESEARCH

There are three ways of addressing the question of whether economics education makes students less pro-social: (1) asking questions about students' attitudes, (2) analysing their behaviour in laboratory experiments, and (3) looking at real-life behaviour.

1. *Survey studies*   As early as 1966, Sawyer (1966) found substantial differences between the attitudes of business students and other students. He concludes that 'business students are more concerned strictly with maximizing their own welfare, disregarding the other's [...]' (p. 414). Others, for example Schein (1967), test the extent to which attitudes change with management education. His results do not show that students change their 'general cynicism' between the beginning and the end of their degrees. Later studies, which are more interested in the impact of ethics courses, found that 'the decisions made by business students were significantly less ethical [...]' than law students (McCabe et al., 1991: 955). A follow-up study shows that business students hardly change their ethical attitudes, whether they take an ethics course or not (McCabe et al., 1994). Similar results for economics students are found by Gandal and Roccas (2000), who analyse the values embraced by economists and non-economists. They identify differences in the value priorities reported by students of economics compared to non-economists, but these differences already emerge before any economics indoctrination can take place. The difficulty with such studies may of course be that telling the truth is of no benefit. Either economists or non-economists may express what they perceive to be appropriate behaviour, while in reality they would have behaved in a totally different way.

2. *Laboratory experiments*   Taking into account some of the shortcomings of surveys, most studies in economics use laboratory experiments to analyse behavioural differences. Students, for example,

play a prisoner's dilemma game and earn the varying amounts of money. In such settings, material incentives exist to behave 'selfishly'. In this academic community, the results of Frank et al. (1993a, 1996) showing that economics education has a negative influence on students' cooperative behaviour (that is, that there is an indoctrination effect of economics) is widely accepted. But the literature on the topic is less uniform than suggested by Frank et al. (1996: 192), who argue that there is 'a heavy burden of proof on those who insist that economics training does not inhibit cooperation'. While Carter and Irons (1991: 174) find that 'economists are born, not made', there are many more experimental studies which do not find a negative effect of economics education on cooperative behaviour (Marwell and Ames, 1981; Frey et al., 1993; Bohnet and Frey, 1995; Seguino et al., 1996; Cadsby and Maynes, 1998; Stanley and Tran, 1998; Frank and Schulze, 2000). Laboratory experiments, however, have their shortcomings. These studies cannot exclude the factor that economists see the experimental setting as 'an IQ test of sorts' (Frank, 1988: 226). Students may play according to the equilibrium learned in their economics classes, but they do not apply it to real-life situations. Therefore, if economists set up economic experiments with other economists to see whether they behave like economists, they should not be surprised if they really do so.

3.   *Field evidence*   Only two of the previous studies on this topic go beyond laboratory experiments. One of them is a 'lost letter' experiment by Yezer et al. (1996), where envelopes containing money are dropped in different classrooms. On the basis of the number of letters returned, the study concludes that economists are even more honest than students of other subjects. However, the authors cannot control for personal characteristics (for example, gender and age) as they do not know who picks up the envelope. A second paper, looking at 'real-world' behaviour, is that of Laband and Beil (1999). They investigate the differences in the professional associations' dues payment, which are income-based but where income is self-reported (hence, the correct amount cannot be enforced). With that in mind, the authors undertake a survey of the members' 'true' income and find that sociologists are more likely to cheat than either economists or political scientists. If the 'monetary' incentives for cheating (owing to different dues) are taken into account, the authors believe that there are no significant differences between professional academics. But there again, this study does not control for personal characteristics. Business students may differ from other students in their composition according to factors such as gender. Were women to behave more pro-socially, we would not observe an effect of business education but of gender composition. In addition, the

setting in the two studies mentioned does not allow discriminating between selection and indoctrination effects when it comes to behavioural differences between economists and non-economists.

To sum up, the evidence about the effect of economics education on students' behaviour is mixed. Most studies are restricted to survey evidence or laboratory experiments, both of which have their shortcomings. In this chapter, the question of whether economists behave less pro-socially can be addressed in a natural setting. As both selection and indoctrination may be at work, it is useful to discriminate between the two hypotheses.

6.2 BEHAVIOURAL HYPOTHESES

If behavioural differences between economists and non-economists can be detected empirically, such differences could be attributed to two effects: selection and indoctrination.

SELECTION HYPOTHESIS: Less pro-social persons choose to study economics. Differences in the pro-social behaviour of economics students and other students are expected to be present at the onset of their studies, without their ever having attended a single lecture in economic theory.

This hypothesis is based on the notion that people differ in their pro-social preferences. With respect to their 'social value orientation' people may be divided, for example, into individualistic, competitive and cooperative types (see Chapter 2 for a discussion of heterogeneity in individuals). According to this hypothesis, 'individualistic' types self-select into business schools, which means that observed behavioural differences would be due to this selection process and not to any effect of economics education. However, there may be another explanation for behavioural differences between economists and other students, which has more serious implications for economics education:

INDOCTRINATION HYPOTHESIS: Economics students are indoctrinated by training in economics theory. It is expected that behavioural difference between economists and others increase during the studies. In other words, the more economics students learn the basis of economics, the more selfishly they behave compared to other students.

Students may, for example, take the 'expected utility theory' (Von Neumann and Morgenstern, 1947) as normative advice for their own behaviour (Jones et al., 1990). Due to their game theoretical education, economics students reduce their expectations about the pro-social behaviour of others. This would also lead to a reduction in their own pro-social behaviour as seen in Chapter 4. More generally speaking, economics and business administration education decreases cooperative behaviour because the training '(a) teaches a language devoid of ethical symbols, (b) provides a set of simplified assumptions about how the world works, and (c) reinforces acceptance of the rational/economic world view' (Daboub et al., 1995: 155). If the indoctrination hypothesis proves valid, economics faculties would be educating their students to be the type of selfish persons they axiomatically assume in their theories. The two hypotheses are not mutually exclusive and have to be tested empirically.

The economics curriculum at the University of Zurich permits controlling for different levels of economic knowledge. Initially, students undertake their *basic study*, which lasts about two years (four semesters). After passing an exam covering basic macro- and microeconomics and business administration theory, they enter the *main phase* of their studies and choose between economics and business administration. After graduating, students may begin their Ph.D. study. Some of the students gain basic economics knowledge in high school. In the analysis this *pre-university knowledge* (in economics) is controlled for.

6.3   ANALYSIS AND RESULTS

The first subsection looks at the raw data, followed by an in-depth analysis of the selection hypothesis and the indoctrination hypothesis. In the following subsection, alternative hypotheses will be tested using data from the survey.

6.3.1   Differences Between Economists and Non-economists: Descriptive Analysis

The raw data clearly show the differences between economists and non-economists. Table 6.1 shows the descriptive statistics for contributions by economists and non-economists who contribute to at least one fund.

Overall, 64.5 per cent of the economists (economics and business students) contribute to at least one fund, compared to 70.2 per cent of the non-economists. This difference is highly statistically significant (*t*-test: $t = 16.20$, $p < 0.001$). This result supports the notion that there are differences in pro-social behaviour between economists and non-economists, and that the differences are quite large. To further detect whether these differences are due to a selection or an indoctrination effect, we have to look at the beginning of the students' careers at the University of Zurich and see how their pro-social behaviour develops throughout their studies. With respect to these questions, Table 6.1 shows three interesting patterns:

Table 6.1   *Proportion of economists and non-economists contributing*

	Contribution to at least one fund	*t*-test of difference
Total		
Economics/business	64.5 (18,603)	$p < 0.01$
Other faculties	70.2 (161,622)	
Freshmen		
Economics/business	70.7 (1,688)	$p < 0.01$
Other faculties	74.5 (11,997)	
Basic stage		
Economics/business	68.3 (7,559)	$p < 0.01$
Other faculties	71.4 (32,667)	
Main stage		
Economics	69.2 (887)	$\Delta_{economics-business}: p < 0.01$
Business	56.8 (5,541)	$\Delta_{economics-others}: p = 0.11$
Other faculties	71.7 (90,703)	$\Delta_{business-others}: p < 0.01$
Ph.D.		
Economics	65.0 (434)	$\Delta_{economics-business}: p = 0.69$
Business	63.9 (1,066)	$\Delta_{economics-others}: p = 0.19$
Other faculties	61.9 (27,685)	$\Delta_{business-others}: p = 0.19$

Notes: Number of observations in parentheses.

Source: University of Zurich, 1998-2002.

1. A big difference already exists at the very beginning of the University programme. Freshmen, before attending a single lecture, differ in a statistically significant way in their behaviour; 74.5 per cent of non-economists contribute, compared to only 70.7 per cent of the economists ($t = 3.35, p < 0.01$). This result seems to support the selection hypothesis.
2. During the main phase of their study, the pro-social behaviour of economics students changes in the same way as for non-economists. The difference between economics students (69.2 per cent) and non-economists (71.7 per cent) is not statistically significant ($t = 1.62, p < 0.105$). For economics students, no indoctrination effect is expected based on the descriptive analysis. Only for business students does the willingness to contribute decrease dramatically. Only 56.8 per cent contribute to the funds, while 71.7 per cent of the non-economists behave pro-socially. The difference of 14 percentage points is statistically significant ($t = 23.68, p < 0.001$). The difference widens, thus supporting the indoctrination hypothesis.

3. During their Ph.D. studies, the differences between business students and non-economists level off. 63.9 per cent of business economists donate money at this stage of their studies, compared to 61.9 per cent of non-economists. The difference is not statistically significant ($t = 1.30$, $p < 0.193$). For business students, this signifies an increase in pro-social behaviour. For non-economists, a respective decrease is observed. This pattern does not fit the indoctrination hypothesis: if a possible indoctrination effect increases according to the number of semesters studied, one would expect Ph.D. students to be most affected. Economics students in their Ph.D. study do not significantly differ from non-economists ($t = 1.31$, $p < 0.192$).

The descriptive analysis clearly supports the selection hypothesis, while showing an unclear picture concerning the indoctrination hypothesis. For economics students no indoctrination effect can be detected by relying on the descriptive statistics. For business students, the willingness to contribute decreases but increases again for people studying for a Ph.D. However, economics students and students of other subjects may of course differ in other respects. Other factors can influence pro-social behaviour besides economics and business training. For example, women are less likely to choose to study economics at the University of Zurich than other subjects (for example, humanities). A potential 'economics education' effect may then be due to the gender composition of the two groups compared. To exclude such alternative interpretations, the next sections control for such factors in a multivariate regression analysis. Firstly, the selection effect is analysed in detail and secondly, the indoctrination effect is studied, using methods to control for individual heterogeneity.

6.3.2   Selection Hypothesis

In order to test whether individuals who choose to study economics behave less pro-socially, a closer look is needed at students' first decision to contribute to the two funds. Table 6.2 presents a probit analysis, which controls for personal characteristics. The dichotomous dependent variable equals 1 if the student contributed to at least one of the two funds and 0 if the students free-ride completely. Because some students acquired economics knowledge in high school, this effect is controlled for using the dummy variable *pre-university knowledge,* which equals 1 if the students had economics in their high school curriculum and 0 otherwise. It also controls for personal characteristics: the dummy variable *gender* equals 1 for women, *nationality* is 1 for foreigners, and *age* is controlled for. As this is a pooled data set, *time dummies* control for the time when the decision was taken.

Because the coefficients in a probit analysis are not easy to interpret, marginal effects are computed. They show how the probability of contribution changes compared to the reference group.

Table 6.2   Contribution of economists and non-economists in the first semester

Dichotomous dependent variable: Contribution to at least one fund (=1)			
Economics/Business Students (=1)	-0.133**	(-3.67)	[-4.4%]
Pre-university knowledge	-0.089**	(-2.97)	[-2.9]
Control variables			
Gender (female = 1)	-0.138**	(-5.72)	[-4.4]
Nationality (foreigner = 1)	-0.003	(-0.07)	[-0.1]
Aged below 26	Reference group		
Aged 26-30	0.028	(0.54)	[0.9]
Aged 31-35	0.115	(1.39)	[3.6]
Aged 36-40	0.213	(1.80)	[6.4]
Aged above 40	0.349*	(2.61)	[9.9]
Constant	0.445**	(14.48)	
Time dummies	Yes		
Number of observations	13,685		
Log likelihood	-7,719.701		

Notes: Coefficients of probit regression. *z*-values in parentheses. Marginal effects in brackets. Reference group consists of 'non-economists', 'without pre-university economic knowledge', 'aged below 26', 'male', 'Swiss', 'winter semester 1998/99'.
Level of significance: * $0.01 < p < 0.05$, ** $p < 0.01$

Source: University of Zurich, 1998-2002.

The results support the selection hypothesis. The probability that an economics student will contribute to one of the funds is 4.4 percentage points lower compared to the reference group of non-economists. The effect is statistically significant ($p < 0.01$). Thus, before attending a single lecture in economics, economics and business students contribute less than other students do in their first semester. The possibility that pre-university knowledge is responsible for the observed behavioural difference can be excluded. However, pre-university knowledge in economics has an effect on contributions. The probability of contributing is 2.9 percentage points lower if students acquired economics knowledge in high school. This effect can either be a selection or an indoctrination effect, but it cannot explain the economics effect. For a discussion of the control variables, see Chapter 3.

At the University of Zurich, students have to attend approximately two years of basic studies in economics *and* business administration. After that, they specialize in economics or business administration. Therefore, it is unknown whether the less pro-social students select economics or business administration. But, in a panel data set, it is possible to observe how students, who later choose one or the other of the two subjects, behaved in their first semester or in their basic study. Table 6.3 shows the relevant numbers for economics and business students who contributed to one of the two funds in either their first semester or the basic study. The descriptive statistic is already striking: business students behave significantly less pro-socially than economics students do. Only 60 per cent of business students contribute when making their first decision, compared to 77 per cent of economics students in their first semester. In the basic study on the whole, the differences remain almost as impressive: 65 per cent of business students contribute to at least one fund, compared to 74 per cent of economics students. Both differences are statistically significant ($p < 0.01$). Less pro-social students tend to choose business administration and not economics.

To sum up, the results show that the behavioural differences can be explained by a selection effect. In their first semester, business students contribute substantially less than non-economists do. Economics students, on the other hand, do not differ from non-economists ($t = 0.385$; $p < 0.700$). However, the indoctrination hypothesis also has to be tested because the hypotheses are not mutually exclusive. In the next section, it is investigated whether the behavioural differences between economists and non-economists are (also) due to their economics training.

Table 6.3   *Contribution of economics and business students as freshmen or in basic stage*

Contribution to at least one fund by ...	Freshmen	Basic study
Economics	76.9 (39)	73.9 (418)
Business	60.1 (203)	65.3 (1,914)
Other faculties	74.2 (13,438)	71.1 (37,905)
Diff. Economics-Business	$t = 1.999$; $p < 0.047$	$t = 3.416$, $p < 0.001$
Diff. Business-Others	$t = 4.557$, $p < 0.001$	$t = 5.441$, $p < 0.001$
Diff. Economics-Others	$t = 0.385$, $p < 0.700$	$t = 1.095$, $p < 0.273$

Notes: Proportion of students contributing. Number of observations in parenthesis. Mann-Whitney tests of the difference between economics freshmen and business freshmen: $z = 1.805$ ($p < 0.071$); and between economics freshmen and other freshmen: $z = 0.296$ ($p < 0.767$).

Source: University of Zurich, 1998-2002.

6.3.3   Indoctrination Hypothesis

It may be conjectured that the more students learn about the basics of economics, such as the maximization of payoffs, the more they personally act in a profit-maximizing way. For those students not confronted with economics theory in every lecture, such a decline in pro-social behaviour should not take place. If the differences in giving behaviour between economics students and students of other disciplines increase with every additional semester, the indoctrination hypothesis cannot be proven false. Table 6.1 reveals an ambiguous picture. While for economics students pro-social behaviour does not change from the basic study to the main phase compared to non-economists, the contribution differential from the basic study to the main phase shows more of a decrease for business students than for non-economists – which would support the indoctrination hypothesis. But in the Ph.D. stage (economics and business) students contribute more than non-economists. If indoctrination linearly influences the behaviour of students, the effect should – *ceteris paribus* – be most obvious at the doctoral level, where the students have absorbed the largest amount of economics training. But to test the indoctrination effect properly, two things have to be borne in mind. Firstly, business students can also differ from non-economists because of other factors that influence giving behaviour (for example, gender or age). A multivariate probit regression controls for such factors. Secondly, students in different phases of their studies can differ from each other in unobservable time-invariant characteristics. Some do not pass the exams after the basic studies, making students in the main phase or the Ph.D. stage a special selection. It seems obvious that Ph.D. students may be an even more special selection and therefore hard to compare with general economics and business students. A conditional logit regression including individual fixed effects controls for such unobserved personal characteristics. The two models are presented in Table 6.4.

Panel I in Table 6.4 presents the probit estimation. The dichotomous dependent variable equals 1 if students contribute to at least one fund and 0 otherwise. The variable *economics and business students* in the estimation again supports the selection hypothesis: economics and business students contribute less to the funds – independent of the phase of study. The probability is 3.3 per cent lower than for non-economists. For economics students, both coefficients in Panel I that reflect a possible indoctrination effect, *main phase*economics students* and *Ph.D.*economics students*, have the wrong sign and are therefore positive and statistically significant at a 90 per cent significance level. This result does not support the indoctrination hypothesis.

Table 6.4   Contribution of economics and business students

Dichotomous dependent variable: Contribution to at least one fund (=1)

Variable	Panel I		Panel II
Economics and business students	-0.092**	[-3.3%]	
	(-6.55)		
Phases of study			
Freshmen	-0.025	[0.9]	-0.347**
	(-1.71)		(-8.13)
Main phase	0.112**	[3.9]	0.166**
	(12.33)		(4.24)
Main phase*economics students	0.093*	[3.1]	-0.186
	(1.99)		(-0.71)
Main phase*business students	-0.226**	[-8.3]	0.200*
	(-10.15)		(2.04)
Ph.D.	-0.023	[-0.8]	0.090
	(-1.77)		(1.10)
Ph.D.*economics students	0.165*	[5.5]	-0.028
	(2.58)		(-0.05)
Ph.D.*business students	0.179**	[5.9]	0.420
	(4.22)		(1.13)
Pre-university economic knowledge	-0.104**	[-3.7]	
	(-12.40)		
Constant	0.158**		
	(7.87)		
Control variables	Yes		Yes
Time dummies	Yes		Yes
Individual fixed effects	No		Yes
Number of observations	180,225		74,982
Log likelihood	-108,370.56		-27,953.98

Notes: Coefficient of a probit regression in panel I. Coefficient of a conditional logit model in Panel II. z-value in parentheses. Marginal effects in brackets. Reference group consists of 'non-economists', 'basic study', 'without pre-university economic knowledge', 'aged below 26', 'male', 'Swiss', 'semester 1998/99'. Control variables are Age, Age squared, Gender, Nationality, Number of semesters, Number of semesters squared.
Level of significance: * $0.01 < p < 0.05$, ** $p < 0.01$.

Source: University of Zurich, 1998-2002.

Panel I supports the inconsistent picture with respect to the indoctrination effect for business students: moving from the basic study to the main phase of university education raises students' pro-social behaviour by 4 percentage points. The coefficient of the dummy for *main phase*business students* measures the differences between business students and non-economists when entering the main phase, and hence also serves as a test for the indoctrination effect. For business students, entering the main phase of their studies lowers the probability of pro-social behaviour by about 8 percentage points – in addition to the general effect for entering the main phase. This effect is statistically significant. Although this result for business students is consistent with the indoctrination hypothesis, the fact that the probability of pro-social behaviour increases for doctoral students of business economics is not. The probability for business students increases about 6 percentage points, which is statistically significant at a 99 per cent level. As mentioned already, one would expect indoctrination to be the most marked at the Ph.D. stage, where students have accumulated the largest amount of economics training. The argument that indoctrination should be highest in the Ph.D. stage assumes, however, that doctoral students differ from other students only in the stage of the studies. But Ph.D. students are perhaps a different selection of people, which also has to be taken into account.

The results and interpretation of the indoctrination effect presented above are problematic in one respect: as already mentioned for Ph.D. students, students in the main phase of their studies can be seen as a particular selection of people compared to students in the basic study, because a large number of students fail to pass the exam enabling them to enter the main phase. Thus, a sample selection bias cannot be excluded in a probit analysis. To eliminate these doubts, the panel structure of the data set is used. The indoctrination effect is tested in a conditional logit model with individual fixed effects. With this method, any selection biases can be excluded by holding unobserved personal characteristics constant.

Panel II in Table 6.4 presents the results of the conditional logit model with individual fixed effects. In this type of model, because only those students are of interest who have at least once changed their pattern of decision-making with respect to contributing to the funds, the sample is reduced to 12,035 persons. These students have decided on average 6.2 times, which leads to 74,982 observations. The model used allows making intrapersonal comparisons. It looks at how individuals change their behaviour when, for example, entering the main phase of studies. Of course, variables, which do not change during the course of their studies, like pre-university knowledge, gender or nationality, have to be excluded from the analysis.

The results do not support the indoctrination hypothesis. Neither of the two coefficients which would measure the effect of economics and business training on pro-social behaviour shows a statistically significant effect of indoctrination. The coefficients of *main phase*business students* and *Ph.D.*business students* even have the wrong sign. For business students, where the largest selection effects should be expected due to the fact that a large proportion either does not pass the exams or does not choose to carry on to Ph.D. level, the results show that it is crucial to control for unobservable time-invariant heterogeneity. In Table 6.A.1 in the Appendix, the results are replicated for different measurements of a potential indoctrination effect, for example whether pro-social behaviour decreases with the number of semesters in economics or business administration.

These estimates also show that, when unobserved heterogeneity is not controlled for, the indoctrination hypothesis cannot be proven false. However, the results of the models with individual fixed effects, which only look at intrapersonal differences, reveal another picture: economics and business education does not have a negative effect on students' willingness to contribute money to the two social funds. This can be shown by looking at the aggregate behaviour of people who are observable in the basic *and* in the main study. It can then be observed whether this group of people changes its actual behaviour. For economics students, 74.1 per cent ($N = 451$) contribute to at least one fund when they are in the basic study and 77.1 per cent ($N = 367$) contribute to the funds when in the main phase. The increase in pro-social behaviour is, however, not statistically significant ($t = 1.009, p < 0.31$). The evidence is also very clear for business students: 64.9 per cent ($N = 2,150$) contribute in the basic study while 67.8 per cent ($N = 1,919$) do so in the main phase. The slight increase in pro-social behaviour is statistically significant ($t = 1.966; p < 0.05$). Neither economics students nor business students change their behaviour when entering the main phase of studies.

The data do *not* support a negative effect of economics education on pro-social behaviour. When possible selection biases are controlled for, no indoctrination effect can be found. The effects of the probit model in Table 6.4 are due to unobserved heterogeneity. Students in the main phase differ from students in the basic or the Ph.D. stage in unobserved personal characteristics. Economics students therefore do not see economic theory as normative advice for pro-social behaviour.

6.3.4 Discussion of Alternative Hypotheses

Three alternative hypotheses are discussed in this section: (1) economics students differ in other dimensions from non-economists (for example, income), which may explain the observed differences; (2) economics students become more sceptical about the efficiency of the fund management and subsequently reduce their contributions; and (3) the expectations about the behaviour of other people change more dramatically for economists during their studies.

Evidence from the on-line survey of the student population allows addressing these three alternative hypotheses.

6.3.4.1   Income situation

Economists' income may differ from students of other subjects, which may in turn explain the behavioural differences. The survey seeks to determine the income situation, assuming that the better off students are, the more likely they are to help others. This hypothesis is based on empirical findings that the percentage of households that donate increases with income, while the percentage of household income devoted to giving to charity is related to income in a u-shaped way (for example, Andreoni, 2002: 11372). However, those students working to help finance their studies (which is a significant number of students at the University of Zurich) are expected to donate less. In a recent study, students decreased their contribution in a dictator game substantially when they had to earn the money, compared to a situation where they received the money from the experimenter (Cherry et al., 2002). In contrast, when parents pay for their studies (and therefore the contribution to the funds), it is likely that students are more generous with respect to their fellow students. Thus a classical low-cost decision situation may occur (Kirchgässner, 1992).

Table 6.5 presents the probit regression which tests the influence of the income situation on giving behaviour. Panel I therefore uses the survey data to replicate the estimations for actual behaviour in order to see whether answers to the survey are biased. The survey results only partially replicate the results of the analysis of the real data. For example, economists report a higher willingness to donate to at least one fund while in reality they have a lower propensity to contribute. As the survey results seem to be biased, the results have to be interpreted with much care. The probability that students of economics contribute to at least one fund decreases in the main phase and increases in the Ph.D. study but the differences are not statistically significant. In comparison, students of business administration give significantly less when they enter the main phase of their studies. The results also hold when controlling for the income situation, which can be seen in Panel II in Table 6.5, where income variables are added. The income situation of economists cannot explain the behavioural differences between economists and non-economists.

The influence of the income situations on pro-social behaviour is mostly as expected. *Income* has a strong positive effect on the probability of contributing to the two funds. As can be seen by the coefficient of the variable *Contribution towards own upkeep*, the more a student finances his or her own living, the less he or she is willing to contribute. Surprisingly, the fact that parents pay the fees (*Parents paying fees*) decreases the willingness to contribute. The change in the contribution probability, however, is not statistically significant. Keeping in mind that the results based on the survey results are biased and not extremely stable, the results of Table 6.5 cannot support the first alternative hypothesis. The income situation of economics and business students cannot explain the difference between economists and non-economists.

Table 6.5   Income factors affecting giving behaviour

Dichotomous dependent variable: Contribution to at least one fund (=1)

	Panel I		Panel II	
Business and economics students	0.061	[1.6%]	0.036	[1.0%]
	(0.50)		(0.295)	
Main phase	0.057	[1.6]	0.050	[1.4]
	(0.74)		(0.649)	
Main phase*economics students	-0.431	[-13.8]	-0.362	[-9.8]
	(-1.62)		(-1.347)	
Main phase*business students	-0.333	[-10.3]	-0.372*	[-10.0]
	(-1.93)		(-2.146)	
Ph.D.	0.019	[0.5]	0.018	[0.5]
	(0.13)		(0.155)	
Ph.D.*economics students	0.404	[9.2]	0.215	[5.8]
	(0.60)		(0.327)	
Ph.D.*business students	0.064	[1.7]	0.016	[0.4]
	(0.13)		(0.031)	
Income (log)			0.207**	[5.6]
			(4.704)	
Contribution (%) towards own upkeep			-0.004**	[-0.1]
			(-3.135)	
Parents paying fees (=1)			-0.123	[-3.5]
			(-1.645)	
Age	0.010	[0.3]	0.006	[0.2]
	(1.49)		(0.754)	
Gender (female = 1)	0.124*	[3.4]	0.138*	[3.7]
	(2.06)		(2.260)	
Number of semesters	-0.013	[-0.4]	-0.013	[-0.3]
	(-1.85)		(-1.778)	
Constant	0.610**		-0.418	
	(3.66)		(1.300)	
Number of observations	2,425		2,425	
Log likelihood	-1,191.37		-1,177.28	

Notes: Coefficients of probit regressions. *z*-values in parentheses. Marginal effects in brackets. Reference group consists of 'non-economists', 'basic study', 'males', who 'pay their fees themselves'.
Level of significance: * $0.01 < p < 0.05$, ** $p < 0.01$.

Source: Own survey, University of Zurich, 2000.

6.3.4.2 Awareness of efficient management

Business students may critically scrutinize the fund managements' efficiency to a greater extent than other students do. With more economics and business education, this may become more pronounced. A lower contribution rate may therefore be due to a higher awareness of the shortcomings of the specialized funds. Economics and business students would then become more sceptical about the effectiveness of the funds with more economics and business education. They also increasingly substitute these particular funds with other charities. In the on-line survey, the students were asked, 'how do you evaluate the effectiveness of the funds?' on a scale from 8 = 'good' to 1 = 'bad' (with a 'no idea' option).

Table 6.6 Perceived efficiency of the two funds

	'How do you evaluate the effectiveness of the funds?' (On a scale from 8 = 'good' to 1 = 'bad')				
	Economics and business students		Other students		t-test of differences
Basic study	4.96	[115]	5.31	[622]	$t = 2.15$
	(1.65)		(1.62)		$p > |t| = 0.05$
Main phase	4.82	[123]	5.31	[877]	$t = 2.79$
	(1.83)		(1.80)		$p > |t| = 0.01$
Ph.D. study	4.56	[16]	4.96	[194]	$t = 0.74$[1]
	(2.34)		(2.03)		$p > |t| = 0.23$
Total	4.87	[254]	5.27	[1693]	$t = 3.37$
	(1.78)		(1.77)		$p > |t| = 0.01$

Notes: Means are computed. Standard deviations in parentheses. Number of observations in brackets. Without the 'No idea' answers.

Source: Own survey, University of Zurich, 2000.

Table 6.6 shows that economics and business students indeed evaluate the funds in a much more critical way than others. The mean for economics and business students is 4.87 compared to 5.27 for others ($t = 3.37; p < 0.01$). The perceived efficiency decreases slightly for economics and business students in the basic and main phases of their studies. However, this decline is not statistically significant at any conventional level ($t = 0.598; p < 0.550$). This supports the selection hypothesis, claiming that economics and business students already differ from others at the beginning of their studies. During their studies, students do not change their attitudes much. This conclusion can be supported by analysing answers to other questions in the same way, for instance the perceived importance of funds, or political orientation. Economics and business students are a special selection of people and education does not change these attitudes. Due to the limitation of the survey, it cannot distinguish between economics and business students in the basic study, so the evidence presented holds only for the two groups taken together. The result does not support the second alternative hypothesis. Economics and business students do not become more sceptical about the efficiency of the two funds during their studies.

6.3.4.3 Expectations about the behaviour of others

One possible channel for the development of an indoctrination effect would be that economic training lowers expectations about the pro-social behaviour of others. This in turn would lower pro-social behaviour (see Chapter 4 about conditional cooperation). To test this development empirically in the survey, students were asked what proportion of students they expected to contribute to the two funds.[2] Although the difference in expectations between economists and non-economists seems to widen during the course of the degree, the differences are not statistically significant at any phase of studies (see Table 6.A.2 in the Appendix). The indoctrination hypothesis can therefore also not be supported by the shaping of expectations. Previous results about economics students' expectations are also ambiguous. While Frank et al. (1993a) find different expectations between economists and non-economists, other studies do not find statistically significant differences (Selten and Ockenfels, 1998; Yezer et al., 1996). The fact that the expectations of economists are not much shaped by economic training in the analysed decision setting is not surprising, because people built expectations out of a real decision situation. The context of the decision situation is a crucial guide in building expectations because either metaphors are involved in their development (see, for example, Allison et al., 1996; Ortmann and Gigerenzer, 1997) or, in the field, contact with others allows for more accurate expectations (Frank, 1988: 140). In laboratory experiments students have to rely much more on theoretical concepts for developing expectations because contextual clues are excluded.[3]

To sum up, the three alternative hypotheses cannot explain differences in contributions to the two social funds at the University of Zurich. Differences in material resources, different levels of awareness of efficiency, and expectations about the behaviour of others cannot explain the differences in pro-social behaviour between economics students and other students. The evidence presented by the on-line survey supports the selection hypothesis even further, showing that business students differ right at the beginning of their studies from other students, but that business education does not change their behaviour afterwards.

6.4   CONCLUSION

This chapter has presented an analysis of the effect of economics education on pro-social behaviour based on field evidence. Three main results can be derived from the empirical analysis. Firstly, there are behavioural differences between economists and non-economists. Economists are less prepared to behave pro-socially, that is to contribute to the two funds at the University of Zurich. Secondly, the differences are due to a selection effect of more selfish people into the discipline of economics. Economics training does not therefore negatively indoctrinate students. Thirdly, 'selfish' types select themselves into business administration. Economics students behave as pro-socially as non-economists.

In order to interpret the results and to put them into a larger context, three remarks have to be made:

1. The most important result of this study shows that economics education does not undermine pro-social behaviour as measured by the contributions to the two social funds. The criticism that economics education produces 'bad' citizens is therefore not supported. However, the results cannot help decide whether introducing ethics courses can strengthen pro-social behaviour. It may be possible that ethics courses for future leaders (for example, in business schools) would have a positive effect on problems like corporate illegal activity. The results by McCabe et al. (1994), however, do not show a positive effect of ethics courses on ethical attitudes.

2. The results are based on a selection of people into different studies. The effect of economics education is therefore measured exclusively for students who choose to study economics. In order to analyse whether such an education has an effect on people's average pro-social behaviour, people should be randomly forced to acquire knowledge in economics. However, the result that economics students do not become indoctrinated is probably more relevant than whether average people are indoctrinated by potential economics training.

3. The evidence about the missing indoctrination effect is limited to charitable contributions. Students do not seem to take basic economics theory as a normative device in such a situation. The question remains whether students in other situations rely more on their theoretical background. It could be assumed that while people's personal behaviour in spontaneous situations is not affected by learned theories, when making decisions (or advising decision-makers) on more abstract situations with long-run consequences people rely on their theoretical background as a guide.[4] Economists may then stress, for example,

efficiency too much over equity. Indoctrination in such situations may have even more severe effects for society. Take the example of pay-for-performance: standard economics decrees that people will undertake an effort only if the incentives are high enough. Economists ought therefore to advise decision-makers that monetary incentives will always increase effort. However, as discussed in the survey part of this book, monetary incentives can have detrimental effects under specific conditions, which are neglected by standard theory. If economists stick to these too simple theoretical relationships when advising decision-makers in the public or the private sphere, the outcome may be negatively influenced by economics training. However, on the one hand, results about how strictly economists would apply the price mechanism in a situation of over-demand do not give a clear picture of economics students being indoctrinated in this respect (Frey et al., 1993; Haucap and Just, 2003). On the other hand, scientists from other faculties may well provide policy advice on a particular theoretical basis which is simplified. Whether the implications of such theories are more accurate than economics theory has to be questioned.

The results in this chapter are important, especially with respect to the recurring demand that more effort should be put into educating economics students to become good citizens. The results show that economics education does not change the citizenship behaviour of the subject's students. Therefore, this branch of criticism about economics theory cannot be supported. Nevertheless, the criticism is right that economics theory is probably too simplified in various respects, which may influence the thinking of economists and their advice to decision-makers.

NOTES

1. The assumption for a t-test of differences is that the error term is normally distributed. However, if the number of observations is not large enough, a non-parametric test is appropriate because no assumption about the distribution of the error term has to be made. A respective Mann-Whitney test of the difference at the Ph.D. stage is also not statistically significant ($z = 0.771$; $p < 0.441$).
2. The question from the on-line questionnaire was used here instead of the guesses in the field experiment because in the field experiment too few observations came from economics students.
3. If students have to think about the optimal strategy in an artificial public good situation and in a dictator game, they more often play the equilibrium strategy (Croson, 2000).
4. Caplan (2002) finds systematic differences in the beliefs of economists and non-economists about the economy. For example, significantly more economists think that it is not a problem for the economy if 'top executives are paid too much'. The general public believes that this may be an important reason why the economy is not doing better.

APPENDIX

Table 6.A.1   Various measurements for economics training

Dichotomous dependent variable: Contribution to at least one fund (=1)

Variables	(1)	(2)	(3)	(4)
Economics and business students	-0.105** (0.017)		-0.099** (0.013)	
Number of economics and business semesters	-0.005** (0.001)	-0.000 (0.012)		
Number of business semesters			-0.011** (0.001)	-0.007 (0.009)
Number of economics semesters			0.005* (0.002)	-0.017 (0.022)
Main phase	0.121** (0.009)	0.234** (0.036)	0.125** (0.009)	0.151 (0.080)
Ph.D. study	0.006 (0.013)	0.145 (0.080)	0.008 (0.013)	0.000 (0.003)
Pre-university economic knowledge	-0.101 (0.008)		-0.101** (0.008)	
Control variables	Yes	Yes	Yes	Yes
Individual fixed effects	No	Yes	No	Yes
Number of observations	180,225		180,225	74,982
Log likelihood	-108,422.16		-108,393.7	-27,992.1

Notes: Panels (1) and (3) show coefficients of probit regressions. Panels (2) and (4) show coefficients of logit regressions. Standard errors in parentheses. Control variables are age, gender, nationality and number of semesters. Reference group consists of 'non-economists', 'basic study', 'without pre-university economic knowledge', 'aged below 26', 'male', 'Swiss', 'semester 1998/99'.
Level of significance: * $0.01 < p < 0.05$, ** $p < 0.01$

Data source: University of Zurich, 1998-2002.

Table 6.A.2   Expectations about the behaviour of others

What percentage of the student population contributes to both funds? (Guess)				
	Economics and business students		Other students	*t*-test
Basic study	69.89	(19.45) [177]	69.74 (18.74) [972]	*p* = 0.46
Main phase	64.46	(19.43) [204]	66.08 (19.85) [1337]	*p* = 0.14
Ph.D. study	60.40	(16.70) [25]	62.45 (19.88) [282]	*p* = 0.31
Total	66.58	(19.48) [406]	67.06 (19.58) [2591]	*p* = 0.32

Notes: Mean guess. Standard deviation in parentheses. Number of observations in brackets. Without the 'No idea' answers. A respective Mann-Whitney test of the difference in the Ph.D. study is also not statistically significant ($z = 0.693$; $p < 0.488$).

Source: Own survey, University of Zurich, 2000.

7. Concluding Remarks

The theoretical and empirical analysis in this book produces good and bad news for individuals living together in social groups. The good news is that the prospect of people behaving pro-socially does not look as gloomy as is often predicted by economic theory. People deviate systematically from the self-interest hypothesis by contributing money and time to public goods. The bad news is that they do not always do so. In certain situations people are not willing to contribute to a good cause and hence the public good is not provided in a socially optimal amount. The important analytical step forward is therefore to isolate the conditions which lead to more and to less pro-social behaviour. The empirical part of this book presents field evidence about the conditions which affect the willingness to contribute money and time to a public good. In the following, the good and the bad news are developed, leading to a consideration of their importance for economic theory and for policy.

Good News: People deviate from the self-interest hypothesis and are willing to behave pro-socially in various settings. The empirical analysis presented in this study is consistent with the findings of previous studies that people are willing to contribute to public goods. Even in an anonymous setting, in which neither selective incentives (for example, a private good or prestige) nor social pressure can explain contribution behaviour, students at the University of Zurich are prepared to donate money to a charity. In contrast to laboratory experiments, the willingness to contribute does not deteriorate dramatically over time.

Bad News: The extent of pro-social behaviour varies with the conditions under which the decision takes place. The bad news arising from the evidence presented in this book is that people are not always prepared to behave pro-socially. There is a large variance in pro-social behaviour. A range of explanations of this variation in contributions is provided by numerous theoretical approaches presented in the survey section. The most promising theories import ideas from psychology or sociology and thereby enrich the economics view of human behaviour. The empirical results presented in this book highlight four important conditions for pro-social behaviour.

1. *Framing effects*   People's pro-social behaviour depends to a large
    extent on institutional framing effects. Small variations in the framing of
    the decision lead to large behavioural effects. For the decision to
    contribute money to two charities at the University of Zurich, a minor
    change in the mode of asking had a tremendous effect on pro-social
    behaviour. The exact mechanism for framing to be effective is still
    underexplored by economics. The frame of the decision probably
    contains information about the social norms of contributing and therefore
    also about the expected intentions of the people involved. On the other
    hand, the frame (or procedure) of a decision can be perceived as fair or
    unfair, which influences one's willingness to behave pro-socially.

2. *Conditional cooperation*   The willingness to behave pro-socially is
    conditional on the behaviour of the reference group. I do not find any
    evidence that people free-ride on the behaviour of others, as expected by
    pure altruism models; rather, they increase their contributions if the
    average group contribution increases. As such, social interaction effects
    are hard to test without an exogenous intervention. In this book, the first
    field experiment was implemented which can systematically address the
    question of how people react to charitable giving by others. The results
    show that people who were informed that many others contributed to the
    two social funds increased their contribution. The most sensitive
    individuals to social interaction effects are those with neither a very
    strong nor a very weak preference for contributing to the two funds. For
    these types of people the information of what others do seems to be more
    important.

    The reason why people vary their individual behaviour with group
    average behaviour has still to be further investigated. Future research
    should try to discriminate between various theoretical explanations and
    investigate the conditions under which various explanations are most
    accurate. From the results of the field experiment it is also not conclusive
    how much a low contribution rate erodes pro-social behaviour. The
    results can be interpreted as meaning that people do not stop contributing
    when informed that only a minority is behaving pro-socially. That would
    imply that either cooperation does not collapse when a majority is free-
    riding or that people have even lower expectations about the behaviour
    of others than assumed. The relevant question remains about the
    conditions under which the behavioural reaction leads to an equilibrium
    with very low pro-social behaviour and when such a cascade does not
    happen.

3. *Monetary incentives*   The price of acting pro-socially has an effect on
    people's behaviour. In order to test the effect of monetary incentives, the
    contributions of the students were matched by 25 per cent or 50 per cent

in a field experiment, which reduced the price of giving. The effect of the field experiment is mostly in line with economic reasoning. For people who are pro-socially inclined, the matching mechanism has the expected effect, but only when the amount matched is large enough. The matching mechanism has no effect on people who never contributed in the past. This result is consistent with the notion that it is extremely difficult to change the behaviour of selfish people. Even if the price of giving is reduced, a material self-interested person thinks that he or she is still better off not contributing to a public good.

Interestingly, the low matching mechanism has no effect on contributions; the results even show a small decrease in the number of people who contribute to at least one of the funds. Such a reduction in giving would support the view that monetary incentives can have detrimental effects on pro-social behaviour. If the normal relative price effect is too small, the motivational crowding effect dominates and pro-social behaviour is reduced. Because the result is not statistically significant and very small, the crowding-out effect of limited donation-matching has to be supported by future studies in order to be conclusive. However, because some sort of intrinsic motivation is a prerequisite for pro-social behaviour, the use of monetary incentives in this area can be problematic. The incentives can, on the one hand, be perceived as controlling and therefore either decrease self-determination or interfere with a trust relationship. On the other hand, the external incentives can make it more difficult for a donor to signal his or her generosity and might therefore reduce his or her donation.

4. *Education*   There is widespread criticism that economics training erodes pro-social behaviour. Especially in recent years, as corporate illegal activities have been uncovered, critics held business schools and economics education at least partly responsible for this unethical behaviour. More generally, it is widely believed that economics training reduces cooperative behaviour. This claim has so far been tested only either by questionnaire studies about attitudes or in laboratory experiments. This book presents the first results based on systematic field evidence to analyse whether economic education has a negative effect on pro-social behaviour. In general, there are large differences between the students of the different faculties, supporting the view that people are heterogeneous in their pro-social preferences. The results show that economics students behave more selfishly than the average non-economists. However, this behavioural difference is due to a selection effect: selfish people choose to study economics. To be precise, selfish persons select business administration in particular. It is therefore not true that 'economists are an unpleasant lot' (*The Economist*, 1993:

71), but that business economists are. The empirical analysis could not detect an indoctrination effect of economics training on top of the selection effect. These means that academic economists do not *create* the type of selfish people (the *homo oeconomicus*) they axiomatically assume in their theories.

The good and the bad news of this book have implications for economic theory. The good news that people behave pro-socially is bad news for orthodox economists, who are reluctant to accept that standard economic theory is limited and sometimes purely wrong in predicting behaviour. Most models are based on assuming that humans strictly maximize their material self-interest. Although these models are very useful for explaining behaviour in a large number of situations, they reach their limits in explaining pro-social behaviour. From a broader perspective, however, additional evidence is always good news, no matter whether it supports or rejects a theory. The respective theory can be modified and as a result better explain real-life behaviour. Thus, to accept the fact that a large majority of people deviate from the self-interest hypothesis and sacrifice time and money for the well-being of others is important for economic theory. If pro-social behaviour is not taken into account, behavioural predictions may be wrong and one of the most interesting and relevant behavioural phenomena cannot be explained.

The insights from the field evidence have to be incorporated into economics models. While the field experiment about matching donations showed that the relative price effect works at least to explain the variance in pro-social behaviour, insights from other social sciences have to be considered to explain the full spectrum of pro-social behaviour. The field evidence supports, for example, the importance of social interaction effects on pro-social behaviour, but future models should seek to explain the conditions under which these motives become more or less pronounced and which situation triggers a particular behavioural pattern.

The empirical results have policy implications for the fostering of pro-social behaviour. Firstly, it is obvious that contributions to public goods are possible without government intervention. It is therefore not necessary for all public goods to be financed by tax money. Moreover, state intervention can act as a substitute for private contributions and therefore produce a classical crowding-out. Moreover, it could be argued that state intervention may even crowd out intrinsic motivations to pro-social behaviour, interfering with self-regulation and resulting in an inferior outcome than without the intervention. The empirical results summarized in the survey part of the book show that while public grants to public goods crowd out private contribution, this classical crowding-out is nonetheless far from being complete. Similarly, the empirical part shows that contributions by others are not perceived as a substitute for one's own contributions. On the contrary, contributions by others increase individuals' pro-social behaviour. With respect to the motivational crowding-out, evidence for the detrimental effects of state intervention is still rare (exceptions are the very interesting results by Cardenas et al., 2000; Frey and Oberholzer-Gee, 1997). However, if these results were to be supported in further studies, state interventions, even if they are designed to induce Pareto-superior outcomes, would have to be evaluated very critically. If they do not take into account potential motivational crowding-effects, the net effect may be contrary to what was intended.

Secondly, the four main results of the empirical analysis allow speculations about how institutions need to be designed in order to foster pro-social behaviour. As discussed above, institutions have to take into account that framing effects are crucially important for pro-social behaviour. The procedures have to be perceived as fair to subsequently increase pro-social behaviour. Similar to pure framing effects, different default settings have huge behavioural effects (see the discussion in Thaler and Sunstein, 2003). It may, for example, be crucial in the case of organ donation whether the default setting is donation (barring explicit opposition) or non-donation (barring explicit approval). Although the decision may seem to be the same, the default as such, presumably set by law, may contain information about either the appropriateness of donating organs or about the quality or risk of donating one's organs. Of course, defaults may also have huge behavioural effects because people procrastinate changing the default setting or suffer some sort of status-quo bias.

Furthermore, people's behaviour is conditional on the behaviour of others. Institutions must therefore avoid instigating a low expectation about the behaviour of others in order to increase pro-social behaviour. People normally underestimate the extent of pro-social behaviour in a group. Depending on the public good, this can be corrected, for instance, by either removing signs of anti-social behaviour or by announcing the donations of other people or of a leader. Many private fundraisers already use this strategy successfully by informing potential donors about how many others have already donated. In the public sphere, there is still much potential for thinking about how to use social interaction effects to increase pro-social behaviour.

The results of the field experiment about matching donations support the notion that monetary incentives work for pro-social behaviour. In the discussion about changing the tax system either by cutting tax rates, introducing a flat-rate income tax or switching to a consumption tax, the effects on charitable giving have to be taken into account. Matching donations can be seen as an alternative method of subsidizing charitable giving. However, as discussed already, the incentives provided under such a model have to be perceived as supportive and not controlling.

The results from the analysis of the relation between economics education and pro-social behaviour suggest that it is very difficult to destroy (and probably also to induce) pro-social behaviour by relying on education. The introduction of more ethics courses in schools may therefore not be a very successful policy for increasing pro-social behaviour. It is also not clear whether the information that helping others makes one happy would persuade people to engage more in voluntary work.

It has become clear in this book, however, that the economic analysis of pro-social behaviour can add insights to a topic that is extremely relevant for the living together of human beings. It is therefore necessary to remain open to the research methods and theoretical approaches of other social sciences. The theoretical predictions gained from such a cooperation of sciences have to be empirically tested in a stringent way – if possible in field settings. Such research would provide a better understanding of the motivations for pro-social behaviour as well as knowledge about how institutions can be designed in order to foster contributions of time and money to public goods.

References

Akerlof, George A. (1982). Labor Contracts as Partial Gift Exchange. *Quarterly Journal of Economics* 97(4). 543-69.

Akerlof, George A. and Rachel E. Kranton (2000). Economics and Identity. *Quarterly Journal of Economics* 115(3). 715-53.

Albert, Max, Werner Güth, Erich Kirchler and Boris Maciejovsky (2002). Are We Nice(r) to Nice(r) People? An Experimental Analysis. *Working Paper*. Max Planck Institute for Research into Economic Systems, Jena.

Alesina, Alberto and Eliana La Ferrara (2000). Participation in Heterogeneous Communities. *Quarterly Journal of Economics* 115(3). 847-904.

Alesina, Alberto and David Dollar (2000). Who Gives Foreign Aid to Whom and Why? *Journal of Economic Growth* 5(1). 33-64.

Alesina, Alberto, Rafael Di Tella and Robert MacCulloch (2004). Inequality and Happiness: Are Europeans and Americans Different? *Journal of Public Economics* 88(9-10). 2009-42.

Allison, Scott T., James K. Beggan and Elizabeth H. Midgley (1996). The Quest for 'Similar Instances' and 'Simultaneous Possibilities': Metaphors in Social Dilemma Research. *Journal of Personality and Social Psychology* 71(3). 479-97.

Alm, James, Gary McClelland and William D. Schulze (1992). Why Do People Pay Taxes? *Journal of Public Economics* 48(1). 21-38.

Almender, Robert (2000). *Human Happiness and Morality: A Brief Introduction to Ethics*. Amherst, New York: Prometheus Books.

Amemiya, Takeshi (1981). Qualitative Response Models: A Survey. *Journal of Economic Literature* 19(4). 1483-536.

Andreoni, James (1988). Privately Provided Public Goods in a Large Economy: The Limits of Altruism. *Journal of Public Economics* 35(1). 57-73.

Andreoni, James (1989). Giving with Impure Altruism: Applications to Charity and Ricardian Equivalence. *Journal of Political Economy* 97(3). 1147-58.

Andreoni, James (1990). Impure Altruism and Donations to Public Goods: A Theory of Warm-glow Giving. *Economic Journal* 100(401). 464-77.

Andreoni, James (1992). Warm-glow Versus Cold-prickle: The Effects of Positive and Negative Framing in Cooperation in Experiments. *Quarterly Journal of Economics* 60(1). 1-21.

Andreoni, James (1993). An Experimental Test of the Public-goods Crowding-out Hypothesis. *American Economic Review* 83(5). 1317-27.

Andreoni, James (1998). Towards a Theory of Charitable Fund-raising. *Journal of Political Economy* 106(6). 1186-213.

Andreoni, James (2002). The Economics of Philanthropy. In: Smelser, Neil J. and Paul B. Baltes (eds). *International Encyclopedia of the Social and Behavioral Sciences*. London: Elsevier. 11369-76.

Andreoni, James (2004). Philanthropy. In: Gérard-Varet, L.A., Kolm, S.C. and J. Mercier Ythier (eds). *Handbook of Giving, Reciprocity and Altruism*. Amsterdam: Elsevier/North Holland. Forthcoming.

Andreoni, James (2005). Leadership Giving in Charitable Fund-raising. *Journal of Public Economic Theory*. Forthcoming.

Andreoni, James and Abigail Payne (2003). Do Government Grants to Private Charities Crowd Out Giving or Fund-raising? *American Economic Review* 93(3). 792-812.

Andreoni, James and John H. Miller (2002). Giving According to GARP: An Experimental Test of the Consistency of Preferences for Altruism. *Econometrica* 70(2). 737-53.

Andreoni, James and John Karl Scholz (1998). An Econometric Analysis of Charitable Giving with Interdependent Preferences. *Economic Inquiry* 36(3). 410-28.

Andreoni, James and Larry Samuelson (2005). Building Rational Cooperation. *Journal of Economic Theory*. Forthcoming.

Andreoni, James and Lise Vesterlund (2001). Which Is the Fair Sex? Gender Differences in Altruism. *Quarterly Journal of Economics* 116(1). 293-312.

Andreoni, James and Ragan Petrie (2004). Public Goods Experiments Without Confidentiality: A Glimpse into Fund-raising. *Journal of Public Economics* 88(7-8). 1605-23.

Andreoni, James, Brian Erard and Jonathan Feinstein (1998). Tax Compliance. *Journal of Economic Literature* 36(2). 818-60.

Andreoni, James, Eleanor Brown and Isaac Rischall (2003). Charitable Giving by Married Couples: Who Decides and Why Does it Matter? *Journal of Human Resources* 38(1). 111-33.

Andreoni, James, William G. Gale and John Karl Scholz (1996). Charitable Contributions of Time and Money. *Working Paper*. University of Wisconsin-Madison.

Anheier, Helmut K. and Lester M. Salamon (1999). Volunteering in Cross-national Perspective: Initial Comparisons. *Law and Contemporary Problems* 62(4). 43-65.

Argyle, Michael (1999). Causes and Correlates of Happiness. In: Kahneman, Daniel, Ed Diener and Norbert Schwarz (eds). *Well-being: The Foundations of Hedonic Psychology*. New York: Russell Sage Foundation. 353-73.

Ashraf, Nava, Iris Bohnet and Nikita Piankov (2002). Decomposing Trust. *Working Paper*. John F. Kennedy School of Government, Harvard University.

Auten, Gerald, Holger Sieg and Charles T. Clotfelter (2002). Charitable Giving, Income and Taxes: An Analysis of Panel Data. *American Economic Review* 92(1). 371-82.

Ball, Sheryl B. and Paula-Ann Cech (1996). Subject Pool Choice and Treatment Effects in Economic Laboratory Research. In: Issac, Mark R. (ed). *Research in Experimental Economics. Volume 6.* 239-92.

Bardsley, Nicholas and Rupert Sausgruber (2002). Social Interaction Effects in the Laboratory and Society: Conformism and Reciprocity in Public Good Provision. *Working Paper*. University of Innsbruck.

Becker, Gary S. (1974). A Theory of Social Interactions. *Journal of Political Economy* 82(6). 1063-93.

Becker, Gary S. (1976). *The Economic Approach to Human Behavior*. Chicago: Chicago University Press.

Bénabou, Roland and Jean Tirole (2002). Intrinsic and Extrinsic Motivation. *Review of Economic Studies* 70. 489-520.

Bénabou, Roland and Jean Tirole (2004). Incentives and Prosocial Behavior. *Working Paper*. Princeton University.

Bertrand, Marianne and Sendhil Mullainathan (2001). Do People Mean What They Say? Implications for Subjective Survey Data. *American Economic Review* 91(2). 67-72.

Bertrand, Marianne, Erzo Luttmer, F.P. and Sendhil Mullainathan (2000). Network Effects and Welfare Cultures. *Quarterly Journal of Economics* 115(3). 1019-55.

Besley, Timothy and Maitreesh Ghatak (2005). Competition and Incentives with Motivated Agents. *American Economic Review* 95(3). 616-36

Bierhoff, Hans-Werner (2002). *Prosocial Behaviour*. New York: Psychology Press.

Blumenthal, Marsha, Charles Christian and Joel Slemrod (2001). Do Normative Appeals Affect Tax Compliance? Evidence from a Controlled Experiment in Minnesota. *National Tax Journal* 54(1). 125-38.

Bohnet, Iris (1997). *Kooperation und Kommunikation: Eine ökonomische Analyse individueller Entscheidungen*. Tübingen: Mohr (Siebeck).

Bohnet, Iris and Bruno S. Frey (1995). Ist Reden Silber und Schweigen Gold? Eine ökonomische Analyse. *Zeitschrift für Wirtschafts- und Sozialwissenschaften* 115. 169-209.

Bohnet, Iris and Bruno S. Frey (1997). Rent Leaving. *Journal of Institutional and Theoretical Economics (JITE)* 153. 711-21.

Bohnet, Iris and Bruno S. Frey (1999a). Social Distance and Other-regarding Behavior in Dictator Games: Comment. *American Economic Review* 89(1). 335-39.

Bohnet, Iris and Bruno S. Frey (1999b). The Sound of Silence in Prisoner's Dilemma and Dictator Games. *Journal of Economic Behavior and Organization* 38(1). 43-57.

Bohnet, Iris and Richard Zeckhauser (2002). Social Comparisons in Ultimatum Bargaining. *Working Paper*. John F. Kennedy School of Government, Harvard University.

Bohnet, Iris and Robert D. Cooter (2003). Expressive Law: Framing or Equilibrium Selection? *Scandinavian Journal of Economics* 106(3). 495-510.

Bohnet, Iris, Bruno S. Frey and Steffen Huck (2001). More Order with Less Law: On Contract Enforcement, Trust and Crowding. *American Political Science Review* 95(1). 131-44.

Bolton, Gary and Axel Ockenfels (2000). ERC – A Theory of Equity, Reciprocity and Competition. *American Economic Review* 90(1). 166-93.

Bolton, Gary and Elena Katok (1998). An Experimental Test of the Crowding Out Hypothesis: The Nature of Beneficent Behavior. *Journal of Economic Behavior and Organization* 37(3). 315-31.

Bolton, Gary E., Elena Katok and Rami Zwick (1998a). Dictator Game Giving: Rules of Fairness Versus Acts of Kindness. *International Journal of Game Theory* 27(2). 269-99.

Bolton, Gary, Jordi Brandts and Axel Ockenfels (1998b). Measuring Motivations for the Reciprocal Responses Observed in a Simple Dilemma Game. *Experimental Economics* 1(3). 207-19.

Bolton, Gary, Jordi Brandts and Elena Katok (2000). How Strategy Sensitive Are Contributions? A Test of Six Hypotheses in a Two-person Dilemma Game. *Economic Theory* 15(2). 367-87.

Bosco, Luigi and Luigi Mittone (1997). Tax Evasion and Moral Constraints: Some Experimental Evidence. *Kyklos* 50(3). 297-324.

Bowles, Samuel, Christina Fong and Herbert Gintis (2004). Reciprocity and Welfare State. In: Gérard-Varet, L.A., S.C. Kolm and J. Mercier Ythier (eds). *Handbook of Giving, Reciprocity and Altruism*. Amsterdam: Elsevier/North Holland.

Brandts, Jordi and Arthur Schram (2001). Cooperation and Noise in Public Goods Experiments: Applying the Contribution Function Approach. *Journal of Public Economics* 79(2). 399-427.

Brennan, Geoffrey and Philip Pettit (1993). Hand Invisible and Intangible. *Synthese* 94. 191-225.

Brown, Eleanor (1999). The Scope of Volunteer Activity and Public Service. *Law and Contemporary Problems* 62(4). 17-42.

Brown, Eleanor and Hamilton Lankford (1992). Gifts of Money and Gifts of Time: Estimating the Effect of Tax Prices and Available Time. *Journal of Public Economics* 47(3). 321-41.

Buraschi, Andrea and Francesca Cornelli (2002). Donations. *Working Paper*. London Business School.

Bütler, Monika (2002). The Political Feasibility of Increasing Retirement Age: Lessons from a Ballot on Female Retirement Age. *International Tax and Public Finance* 9. 349-65.

Cadsby, Charles Bram and Elizabeth Maynes (1998). Choosing Between a Socially Efficient and Free-riding Equilibrium: Nurses Versus Economics and Business Students. *Journal of Economic Behavior and Organization* 37(2). 183-92.

Camerer, Colin (2003). *Behavioral Game Theory*. Princeton: Princeton University Press.

Camerer, Colin and Richard H. Thaler (1995). Anomalies: Ultimatums, Dictators and Manners. *Journal of Economic Perspectives* 9(2). 209-19.

Cameron, Lisa A. (1999). Raising the Stakes in the Ultimatum Game: Experimental Evidence from Indonesia. *Economic Inquiry* 37(1). 47-59.

Caplan, Brian (2002). Systematically Biased Beliefs About Economics: Robust Evidence of Judgmental Anomalies from the Survey of Americans and Economists on the Economy. *Economic Journal* 112(479). 433-58.

Caplan, Brian (2003). Stigler-Becker versus Myers-Briggs: Why Preferences-based Explanations Are Scientifically Meaningful and Empirically Important. *Journal of Economic Behavior and Organization* 50. 391-405.

Cardenas, Juan Camilo, John Stranlund and Cleve Willis (2000). Local Environmental Control and Institutional Crowding-out. *World Development* 28(10). 1719-33.

Carpenter, Jeffrey, Stephen Burks and Eric Verhoogen (2005). Comparing Students to Workers: The Effect of Stakes, Social Framing, and Demographics on Bargaining Outcomes. In: Carpenter, J., G. Harrison and J. List. *Field Experiments in Economics*. Amsterdam: Elsevier/North Holland. 261-90.

Carter, John R. and Michael D. Irons (1991). Are Economists Different, and If So, Why? *Journal of Economic Perspectives* 5(2). 171-7.

Charness, Gary and Brit Grosskopf (2001). Relative Payoffs and Happiness: An Experimental Study. *Journal of Economic Behavior and Organization* 45(3). 301-28.

Charness, Gary and Matthew Rabin (2002). Social Preferences: Some Simple Tests and a New Model. *Quarterly Journal of Economics* 117(3). 817-69.

Cherry, Todd L., Peter Frykblom and Jason F. Shogren (2002). Hardnose the Dictator. *American Economic Review* 92(4). 1218-21.

Cialdini, Robert B. (1993). *Influence: The Psychology of Persuasion.* New York: William Morrow & Company.

Cialdini, Robert B. and Noah J. Goldstein (2004). Social Influence: Compliance and Conformity. *Annual Review of Psychology* 55. 591-621.

Cialdini, Robert B., Douglas T. Kenrick and Donald J. Baumann (1982). Effects of Mood on Prosocial Behavior in Children and Adults. In: Eisenberg, N. (ed.). *The Development of Prosocial Behavior.* New York: Academic Press. 339-59.

Clark, Andrew E. and Andrew J. Oswald (1994). Unhappiness and Unemployment. *Economic Journal* 104(424). 648-59.

Clotfelter, Charles T. (1980). Tax Incentives and Charitable Giving: Evidence of a Panel of Taxpayers. *Journal of Public Economics* 13(3). 319-40.

Clotfelter, Charles T. (1997). The Economics of Giving. In: Barry, John W. and Bruno V. Manno (eds). *Giving Better, Giving Smarter.* Washington, DC: National Commission on Philanthropy and Civic Renewal. 31-55.

Clotfelter, Charles T. (2003). Alumni Giving to Elite Private Colleges and Universities. *Economics of Education Review* 22(2). 109-20.

Coleman, James S. (1990). *Foundations of Social Theory.* Cambridge, MA: Harvard University Press.

Collard, David (1978). *Altruism and the Economy: A Study of Non-selfish Economics.* London: Martin Robertson.

Conlin, Michael, Michael Lynn and Ted O'Donoghue (2003). The Norm of Restaurant Tipping. *Journal of Economic Behavior and Organization* 52(3). 297-321.

Cookson, Richard (2000). Framing Effects in Public Goods Experiments. *Experimental Economics* 3(1). 55-79.

Cornes, Richard and Todd Sandler (1994). Easy Riders, Joint Production, and Public Goods. *Economic Journal* 94(375). 580-98.

Croson, Rachel (1998). Theories of Commitment, Altruism and Reciprocity: Evidence from Linear Public Good Games. *Working Paper.* Wharton School of the University of Pennsylvania.

Croson, Rachel (2000). Thinking Like a Game Theorist: Factors Affecting the Frequency of Equilibrium Play. *Journal of Economic Behavior and Organization* 41(3). 299-314.

Croson, Rachel and Uri Gneezy (2005). Gender Differences in Preferences. *Working Paper.* University of Pennsylvania.

Csikszentmihalyi, Mihaly (1990). *Flow: The Psychology of Optimal Experience.* New York: Harper Perennial.

Daboub, Anthony J., Abdul M.A. Rasheed, Richard L. Priem and David A. Gray (1995). Top Management Team Characteristics and Corporate Illegal Activities. *Academy of Management Review* 20(1). 138-70.

Davis, Douglas D., Edward Millner and Robert Reilly (2005). Subsidy Schemes and Charitable Contributions: A Closer Look. *Experimental Economics* 8(2). 85-106.

Davis, Lance and Douglass C. North (1971). *Institutional Change and American Economic Growth.* New York: Cambridge University Press.

Dawes, Robyn M. and Richard Thaler (1988). Anomalies: Cooperation. *Journal of Economic Perspectives* 2(3). 187-97.

Dawes, Robyn M., Jeanne McTavish and Harriet Shaklee (1977). Behavior, Communication, and Assumptions about other People's Behavior in a Commons Dilemma Situation. *Journal of Personality and Social Psychology* 35(1). 1-11.

Deci, Edward L. (1975). *Intrinsic Motivation.* New York: Plenum Press.

Deci, Edward L. and Richard M. Ryan (1985). *Intrinsic Motivation and Self-determination in Human Behavior.* New York: Plenum Press.

Deci, Edward L. and Richard M. Ryan (1980). The Empirical Exploration of Intrinsic Motivational Processes. *Advances in Experimental Social Psychology* 10. 39-80.

Deci, Edward L., Richard Koestner and Richard M. Ryan (1999). A Meta-analytic Review of Experiments Examining the Effects of Extrinsic Rewards on Intrinsic Motivation. *Psychological Bulletin* 125(6). 627-68.

Di Tella, Rafael, Robert J. MacCulloch and Andrew J. Oswald (2001). Preferences over Inflation and Unemployment: Evidence from Surveys of Happiness. *American Economic Review* 91(1). 335-41.

Diekmann, Andreas (1995). Umweltbewusstsein oder Anreizstrukturen? Empirische Befunde zum Energiesparen, der Verkehrsmittelwahl und zum Konsumverhalten. In: Dieckmann, Andreas and Axel Franzen (eds). *Kooperatives Umwelthandeln: Modelle, Erfahrungen, Massnahmen.* Chur und Zürich: Rüegger. 39-68.

Diekmann, Andreas and Peter Preisendörfer (2003). Green and Greenback: The Behavioral Effects of Environmental Attitudes in Low-cost and High-cost Situations. *Rationality and Society* 15(4). 441-72.

Diener, Ed, Eunkook M. Suh, Richard E. Lucas and Heidi L. Smith (1999). Subjective Well-Being: Three Decades of Progress. *Psychological Bulletin* 125(2). 276-303.

Duncan, Brian (1999). Modeling Charitable Contributions of Time and Money. *Journal of Public Economics* 72(2). 213-42.

Duncan, Brian (2004). A Theory of Impact Philanthropy. *Journal of Public Economics* 88(9-10). 2159-80.

Easterlin, Richard A. (1974). Does Economic Growth Improve the Human Lot? Some Empirical Evidence. In: David, Paul A. and Melvin W. Reder (eds). *Nations and Households in Economic Growth: Essays in Honor of Moses Abramowitz*. New York: Academic Press. 89-125.

Easterlin, Richard A. (ed.) (2002). *Happiness in Economics*. Cheltenham, UK and Northampton, MA, USA: Edward Elgar.

Eckel, Catherine C. and Philip J. Grossman (1996a). Altruism and Anonymous Dictator Games. *Games and Economic Behavior* 16(2). 181-91.

Eckel, Catherine C. and Philip J. Grossman (1996b). The Relative Price of Fairness: Gender Differences in a Punishment Game. *Journal of Economic Behavior and Organization* 30(2). 143-58.

Eckel, Catherine C. and Philip J. Grossman (1997). Are Women less Selfish than Men? Evidence from Dictator Experiments. *The Economic Journal* 108(448). 726-35.

Eckel, Catherine C. and Philip J. Grossman (2001). Differences in the Economic Decisions of Men and Women: Experimental Evidence. In: Plott, Charles R. and Vernon L. Smith (eds). *Handbook of Experimental Economics Results*. Amsterdam: North Holland/Elsevier. Forthcoming.

Eckel, Catherine C. and Philip J. Grossman (2003). Rebate Versus Matching: Does How We Subsidize Charitable Contributions Matter? *Journal of Public Economics* 87(3-4). 681-701.

Eckel, Catherine C. and Philip J. Grossman (2005). Subsidizing Charitable Contributions: A Field Test Comparing Matching and Rebate Subsidies. *Working Paper*. Virginia Polytechnic Institute and Station University.

Economist, The (1993). How Do You Mean 'Fair'? *The Economist*, March 29. 71.

Eichenberger, Reiner and Felix Oberholzer-Gee (1998). Rational Moralists. The Role of Fairness in Democratic Economic Policy. *Public Choice* 94(1-2). 191-210.

Eisenberger, Robert and Judy Cameron (1996). Detrimental Effects of Reward. Reality or Myth? *American Psychologist* 51(11). 1153-66.

Elliott, Catherine S. and Donald M. Hayward (1998). The Expanding Definition of Framing and Its Particular Impact on Economic Experimentation. *Journal of Socio-Economics* 27(2). 229-43.

Elliott, Catherine S., Donald M. Hayward and Sebastian Canon (1998). Institutional Framing: Some Experimental Evidence. *Journal of Economic Behavior and Organization* 35(4). 455-64.

Falk, Armin (2003). Charitable Giving as a Gift Exchange: Evidence from a Field Experiment. *Working Paper*. University of Zurich.

Falk, Armin and Andrea Ichino (2003). Clean Evidence on Peer Pressure. *Journal of Labor Economics*. Forthcoming.

Falk, Armin and Urs Fischbacher (2001). A Theory of Reciprocity. *Games and Economic Behavior*. Forthcoming.

Falk, Armin, Urs Fischbacher and Simon Gächter (2003). Living in Two Neighborhoods – Social Interactions in the Lab. *Working Paper*. University of Zurich.

Farrel, Joseph and Matthew Rabin (1996). Cheap Talk. *Journal of Economic Perspectives* 10(3). 103-18.

Fehr, Ernst and John A. List (2004). The Hidden Costs and Returns of Incentives – Trust and Trustworthiness among CEOs. *Journal of the European Economic Association* 2(5). 743-71.

Fehr, Ernst and Bettina Rockenbach (2003). Detrimental Effects of Sanctions on Human Altruism. *Nature* 422(13). 137-40.

Fehr, Ernst and Klaus M. Schmidt (2003). Theories of Fairness and Reciprocity – Evidence and Economic Applications. In: Dewatripont, Mathias, Lars P. Hansen and Stephen J. Turnovsky (eds). *Advances in Economics and Econometrics - 8th World Congress, Econometric Society Monographs*. Cambridge: Cambridge University Press. 208-57.

Fehr, Ernst and Klaus Schmidt (1999). A Theory of Fairness, Competition, and Cooperation. *Quarterly Journal of Economics* 114(3). 817-68.

Fehr, Ernst and Simon Gächter (1998). Reciprocity and Economics. The Economic Implications of Homo Reciprocans. *European Economic Review* 42(3-5). 845-59.

Fehr, Ernst and Simon Gächter (2000a). Cooperation and Punishment in Public Goods Experiments. *American Economic Review* 90(4). 980-94.

Fehr, Ernst and Simon Gächter (2000b). Fairness and Retaliation: The Economics of Reciprocity. *Journal of Economic Perspectives* 14(3). 159-81.

Fehr, Ernst and Simon Gächter (2002). Do Incentives Contracts Undermine Voluntary Cooperation? *Working Paper*. University of Zurich.

Fehr, Ernst and Urs Fischbacher (2002). Why Social Preferences Matter – The Impact of Non-Selfish Motives on Competition, Cooperation and Incentives. *Economic Journal* 112(478). 1-33.

Fehr, Ernst, Simon Gächter and Georg Kirchsteiger (1997). Reciprocity as a Contract Enforcement Device. *Econometrica* 65(4). 833-60.

Fehr, Ernst, Urs Fischbacher and Elena Tougareva (2002). Do High Stakes and Competition Undermine Fairness? Evidence from Russia. *Working Paper*. University of Zurich.

Fehr, Ernst, Urs Fischbacher, Bernhard von Rosenbladt, Jürgen Schupp and Gert G. Wagner (2002). A Nation-wide Laboratory: Examining Trust and Trustworthiness by Integrating Behavioral Experiments into Representative Surveys. *Smollers Jahrbuch* 122(4). 519-42

Fischbacher, Urs, Simon Gächter and Ernst Fehr (2001). Are People Conditionally Cooperative? Evidence from a Public Goods Experiment. *Economics Letters* 71(3). 397-404.

Fleishman, John A. (1988). The Effects of Decision Framing and Others' Behavior on Cooperation in a Social Dilemma. *Journal of Conflict Resolution* 32(1). 162-80.

Fong, Christina (2001). Social Preferences, Self-interest, and the Demand for Redistribution. *Journal of Public Economics* 82(2). 225-46.

Fong, Christina (2003). Empathic Responsiveness: Evidence from a Randomized Experiment on Giving to Welfare Recipients. *Working Paper*. Carnegie Mellon University.

Frank, Björn and Günther Schulze (2000). Does Economics Make Citizens Corrupt? *Journal of Economic Behavior and Organization* 43(1). 101-13.

Frank, Robert H. (1988). *Passions with Reason: The Strategic Role of the Emotions*. New York: Norton.

Frank, Robert H., Thomas D. Gilovich and Dennis T. Regan (1996). Do Economists Make Bad Citizens? 10(1). 187-92.

Frank, Robert H., Thomas Gilovich and Dennis T. Regan (1993a). Does Studying Economics Inhibit Cooperation? *Journal of Economic Perspectives* 7(2). 159-71.

Frank, Robert H., Thomas Gilovich and Dennis T. Regan (1993b). The Evolution of One-Shot Cooperation: An Experiment. *Ethology and Sociobiology* 14. 247-56.

Freeman, Richard B. (1997). Working for Nothing: The Supply of Volunteer Labor. *Journal of Labor Economics* 15(1). 140-66.

Frey, Bruno S. (1993). Shirking or Work Morale? The Impact of Regulating. *European Economic Review* 37(8). 1523-32.

Frey, Bruno S. (1997a). *Not Just for The Money: An Economic Theory of Personal Motivation.* Cheltenham, UK and Brookfield, USA: Edward Elgar.

Frey, Bruno S. (1997b). A Constitution for Knaves Crowds Out Civic Virtues. *Economic Journal* 107(443). 1043-53.

Frey, Bruno S. (1999). *Economics as a Science of Human Behaviour*. Boston and Dordrecht: Kluwer.

Frey, Bruno S. (2000). *Arts and Economics*. Heidelberg and New York: Springer Verlag.

Frey, Bruno S. (2002). How Does Pay Influence Motivation? In: Frey, Bruno S. and Margit Osterloh (eds). *Successful Management by Motivation: Balancing Intrinsic and Extrinsic Incentives*. Berlin: Springer. 59-88.

Frey, Bruno S. and Alois Stutzer (2000). Happiness, Economy and Institutions. *Economic Journal* 110(446). 918-38.

Frey, Bruno S. and Alois Stutzer (2002a). *Happiness and Economics: How the Economy and Institutions Affect Well-being.* Princeton and Oxford: Princeton University Press.

Frey, Bruno S. and Alois Stutzer (2002b). What Can Economists Learn from Happiness Research? *Journal of Economic Literature* 40(2). 402-35.

Frey, Bruno S. and Alois Stutzer (2003a). Testing Theories of Happiness. *Working Paper.* University of Zurich.

Frey, Bruno S. and Alois Stutzer (2003b). Economic Consequences of Mispredicting Utility. *Working Paper.* University of Zurich.

Frey, Bruno S. and Felix Oberholzer-Gee (1997). The Cost of Price Incentives: An Empirical Analysis of Motivation Crowding-out. *American Economic Review* 87(4). 746-55.

Frey, Bruno S. and Friedrich Schneider (1986). Competing Models of International Lending Activities. *Journal of Development Economics* 20(2). 225-45.

Frey, Bruno S. and Iris Bohnet (1995). Institutions Affect Fairness: Experimental Investigations. *Journal of Institutional and Theoretical Economics* 151(2). 286-303.

Frey, Bruno S. and Lorenz Götte (1999) Does Pay Motivate Volunteers? *Working Paper.* University of Zurich.

Frey, Bruno S. and Matthias Benz (2000). Motivation Transfer Effect. *Working Paper.* University of Zurich.

Frey, Bruno S. and Reto Jegen (2001). Motivation Crowding Theory: A Survey of Empirical Evidence. *Journal of Economic Surveys* 5(5). 589-611.

Frey, Bruno S., Matthias Benz and Alois Stutzer (2004). Introducing Procedural Utility: Not only What, but also How Matters. *Journal of Institutional and Theoretical Economics* 160(3). 377-401.

Frey, Bruno S., Werner W. Pommerehne and Beat W. Gygi (1993). Economics Indoctrination or Selection? Some Empirical Results. *Journal of Economic Education* 24(3). 271-81.

Fudenberg, Drew and Eric Maskin (1986). The Folk Theorem in Repeated Games with Discounting or with Incomplete Information. *Econometrica* 54(3). 533-54.

Gächter, Simon and Arno Riedl (2003). Moral Property Rights in Bargaining with Infeasible Claims. *Working Paper.* University of Amsterdam.

Gandal, Neil and Sonia Roccas (2000). Good Neighbors/Bad Citizens: Personal Value Priorities of Economist. *Working Paper.* Foerder Institute.

Gates, William H. and Chuck Collins (2002). Tax the Wealthy: Why America Needs the Estate Tax. *The American Prospect* 13(11).

Glaeser, Edward L. and José A. Scheinkman (2001). Measuring Social Interaction. In: Durlauf, Steven and Peyton Young (eds). *Social Dynamics.* Cambridge: The MIT Press. 83-131.

Glaeser, Edward L., Bruce Sacerdote and José A. Scheinkman (1996). Crime and Social Interactions. *Quarterly Journal of Economics* 111(2). 507-48.

Glaeser, Edward L., David I. Laibson, José A. Scheinkman and Christine L. Soutter (2000). Measuring Trust. *Quarterly Journal of Economics* 115(3). 811-46.

Glazer, Amihai and Kai A. Konrad (1996). A Signaling Explanation of Charity. *American Economic Review* 86(4). 1019-28.

Gneezy, Uri (2003). The W Effect of Incentives. *Working Paper.* University of Chicago Graduate School of Business.

Gneezy, Uri and Aldo Rustichini (2000). Pay Enough or Don't Pay at All. *Quarterly Journal of Economics* 115(3). 791-810.

Gouldner, Alvin Ward (1960). The Norm of Reciprocity: A Preliminary Statement. *American Sociological Review* 25. 161-78.

Greene, William H. (1997). *Econometric Analysis.* Upper Saddle River, NJ: Prentice Hall.

Gruber, Jonathan and Sendhil Mullainathan (2002). Do Cigarette Taxes Make Smokers Happier? *Advances in Economic Analysis & Policy* 5(1). Article 4.

Harbaugh, William T. (1998a). What Do Donations Buy? A Model of Philanthropy Based on Prestige and Warm Glow. *Journal of Public Economics* 67(2). 169-284.

Harbaugh, William T. (1998b). The Prestige Motive for Making Charitable Transfers. *American Economic Review* 88(2). 277-82.

Hardin, Garrett (1968). The Tragedy of the Commons. *Science* 162. 1243-8.

Harris, Mary B. and Robert J. Smith (1975). Mood and Helping. *The Journal of Psychology* 91(2). 215-21.

Haucap, Justus and Tobias Just (2003). Not Guilty? Another Look at the Nature and Nurture of Economics Students. *Working Paper.* Deutsche Bank.

Heldt, Tobias (2005). Conditional Cooperation in the Field: Cross-Country Skiers' Behavior in Sweden. *Working Paper.* Uppsala University.

Henrich, Joseph, Robert Boyd, Sam Bowles, Colin Camerer, Herbert Gintis, Richard McElreath and Ernst Fehr (2001). In Search of Homo Economicus: Experiments in 15 Small-scale Societies. *American Economic Review* 91(2). 73-79.

Hewstone, Miles, Mark Rubin and Hazel Willis (2002). Intergroup Bias. *Annual Review of Psychology* 53(1). 575-604.

Hoffman, Elisabeth, Kevin McCabe and Vernon Smith (1996). Social Distance and Other-regarding Behavior in Dictator Games. *American Economic Review* 86(3). 653-60.

Hoffman, Elizabeth and Matthew L. Spitzer (1985). Entitlements, Rights and Fairness: An Experimental Examination of Subjects' Concepts of Distributive Justice. *Journal of Legal Studies* 14. 259-97.

Houser, Daniel and Robert Kurzban (2002). Revisiting Kindness and Confusion in Public Goods Experiments. *American Economic Review* 92(4). 1062-9.

Houser, Daniel and Robert Kurzban (2003). Conditional Cooperation and Group Dynamics: Experimental Evidence from a Sequential Public Good Game. *Working Paper*. George Mason University.

Isaac, R. Mark, Deborah Mathieu and Edward E. Zajac (1991). Institutional Framing and Perceptions of Fairness. *Constitutional Political Economy* 2(3). 329-70.

Isen, Alice M. and Paula F. Levin (1972). Effect of Feeling Good on Helping: Cookies and Kindness. *Journal of Personality and Social Psychology* 21(3). 384-8.

Jenni, Karen E. and George Loewenstein (1997). Explaining the Identifiable Victim Effect. *Journal of Risk and Uncertainty* 14(3). 235-57.

Johannesson, Magnus and Björn Persson (2000). Non-reciprocal Altruism in Dictator Games. *Economics Letters* 69(2). 137-42.

Jones, Thomas M., Tom E. Thomas, Bradley R. Agle and Jenifer Ehreth (1990). Graduate Business Education and the Moral Development of MBA Students. Proceedings of the First Annual Meeting of the International Association for Business and Society. 43-53.

Kahan, Dan M. (2002). The Logic of Reciprocity: Trust, Collective Action, and Law. *Working Paper*. Public Law & Legal Theory No. 31, Yale Law School.

Kahneman, Daniel, Ed Diener and Norbert Schwarz (eds) (1999). *Well-being: The Foundations of Hedonic Psychology*. New York: Russell Sage Foundation.

Kaplan, Steven E. and Philip M. Reckers (1985). A Study of Tax Evasion Judgments. *National Tax Journal* 38(1). 97-102.

Kasser, Tim and Richard M. Ryan (2001). Be Careful What You Wish For: Optimal Functioning and the Relative Attainment of Intrinsic and Extrinsic Goals. In: Schmuck, Peter and Kennon M. Sheldon (eds). *Life Goals and Well-being. Towards a Positive Psychology of Human Striving*. Kirkland, WA: Hogrefe and Huber. 116-31.

Kelley, Harold H. and Anthony J. Stahelski (1970). Social Interaction Basis of Cooperators' and Competitors' Beliefs about Others. *Journal of Personality and Social Psychology* 16(1). 66-91.

Kelman, Steven (1987). 'Public Choice' and Public Spirit. *The Public Interest* 87. 80-94.

Keser, Claudia and Frans van Winden (2000). Conditional Cooperation and Voluntary Contributions to Public Goods. *Scandinavian Journal of Economics* 102(1). 23-39.

Khanna, Jyoti and Todd Sandler (2000). Partners in Giving: The Crowding-in Effects of UK Government Grants. *European Economic Review* 44(8). 1543-56.

Kingma, Bruce R. (1989). An Accurate Measurement of the Crowding-out Effect, Income Effect, and Price Effect for Charitable Contributions. *Journal of Political Economy* 97(5). 1197-207.

Kirchgässner, Gebhard (1992). Towards a Theory of Low-cost Decisions. *European Journal of Political Economy* 8. 305-20.

Kollock, Peter (1998). Transforming Social Dilemmas: Group Identity and Co-operation. In: Danielson, Peter A. (ed.). *Modeling Rationality, Morality and Evolution*. New York: Oxford University Press. 186-210.

Kolm, Serge-Chistophe (2000). The Theory of Reciprocity, Giving and Altruism. In: Gérard-Varet, Louis André, Serge-Christophe Kolm and Jean Mercier Ythier (eds). *The Economics of Reciprocity, Giving and Altruism*. Houndmills et al.: Macmillan Press Ltd. 1-44.

Konow, James (2000). Fair Shares: Accountability and Cognitive Dissonance in Allocation Decisions. *American Economic Review* 90(4). 1072-91.

Konow, James (2003a). Conditional versus Unconditional Altruism: Theory and Evidence. *Working Paper*. Loyola Marymount University.

Konow, James (2003b). Which Is the Fairest One of All? A Positive Analysis of Justice Theories. *Journal of Economic Literature* 41(4). 1188-239.

Konow, James and Joseph Earley (2002). The Hedonistic Paradox: Is Homo Economicus Happier? *Working Paper*. Loyola Marymount University.

Kreps, David M., Paul Milgrom, John Roberts and Robert Wilson (1982). Rational Cooperation in the Finitely Repeated Prisoner's Dilemma. *Journal of Economic Theory* 27(2). 245-52.

Kurzban, Robert, Kevin McCabe, Vernon L. Smith and Bart J. Wilson (2001). Incremental Commitment and Reciprocity in a Real-time Public Goods Game. *Personality and Social Psychology Bulletin* 27(12). 1662-73.

Laband, David N. and Richard O. Beil (1999). Are Economists More Selfish Than Other 'Social' Scientists? *Public Choice* 100(1-2). 85-101.

Laibson, David (1997). Golden Eggs and Hyperbolic Discounting. *Quarterly Journal of Economics* 112(2). 443-77.

Lazear, Edward (2000a). Economic Imperialism. *Quarterly Journal of Economics* 115(1). 99-146.

Lazear, Edward P. (2000b). Performance Pay and Productivity. *American Economic Review* 90(5). 1346-61.

Ledyard, John O. (1995). Public Goods: A Survey of Experimental Research. In: Kagel, John and Alvin E. Roth (eds). *Handbook of Experimental Economics*. Princeton: Princeton University Press. 111-94.

Lepper, Mark R. and David Greene (eds) (1978). *The Hidden Costs of Reward: New Perspectives on Psychology of Human Motivation*. Hillsdale, NY: Erlbaum.

Lepper, Mark R., Jennifer Henderlong and Isabelle Gingras (1999). Understanding the Effects of Extrinsic Rewards on Intrinsic Motivation – Uses and Abuses of Meta-analysis: Comment on Deci, Koestner and Ryan (1999). *Psychological Bulletin* 125(6). 669-76.

Levi, Margaret (1988). *Of Rule and Revenue*. Berkeley: University of California Press.

Liebrand, Wim B. (1984). The Effect of Social Motives, Communication and Group Size on Behaviour in an N-person Multi Stage Mixed Motive Game. *European Journal of Social Psychology* 14(3). 239-364.

Lindenberg, Siegwart (1992). An Extended Theory of Institutions and Contractual Discipline. *Journal of Institutional and Theoretical Economics* 148(1). 125-54.

List, John A. and Daniel Rondeau (2003). The Impact of Challenge Gifts on Charitable Giving: An Experimental Investigation. *Economics Letters* 79(2). 153-59.

List, John A. and David Lucking-Reiley (2002). The Effects of Seed Money and Refunds on Charitable Giving: Experimental Evidence from a University Capital Campaign. *Journal of Political Economy* 110(1). 215-33.

Loewenstein, George (2000). Emotions in Economic Theory and Economic Behavior. *American Economic Review* 90(2). 426-32.

Loewenstein, George, Ted O'Donoghue and Matthew Rabin (2003). Projection Bias in Predicting Future Utility. *Quarterly Journal of Economics* 118(4). 1209-48.

Long, Stephen H. (1976). Social Pressure and Contributions to Health Charities. *Public Choice* 28(2). 56-66.

Ludwig, J., G.J. Duncan and P. Hirschfield (2001). Urban Poverty and Juvenile Crime: Evidence from a Randomized Housing-mobility Experiment. *Quarterly Journal of Economics* 116(2). 655-80.

Luttmer, Erzo, F.P. (2001). Group Loyalty and the Taste of Redistribution. *Journal of Political Economy* 109(3). 500-528.

Mael, Fred and Blake E. Ashforth (1992). Alumni and Their Alma Mater: A Partial Test of the Reformulated Model of Organizational Identification. *Journal of Organizational Behavior* 13. 103-23.

Manski, Charles (1993). Identification of Endogenous Social Effects: The Reflection Problem. *Review of Economic Studies* 60(3). 531-42.

Manski, Charles (2000). Economic Analysis of Social Interactions. *Journal of Economic Perspectives* 14(3). 115-36.

Marks, Gary and Norman Miller (1987). Ten Years of Research on the False-consensus Effect: An Empirical and Theoretical Review. *Psychological Bulletin* 102(1). 72-90.

Marwell, Gerald and Ruth E. Ames (1981). Economists Free Ride, Does Anyone Else? Experiments on the Provision of Public Goods IV. *Journal of Public Economics* 15(3). 295-310.

McCabe, Donald L., Janet M. Dukerich and Jane E. Dutton (1991). Context, Values and Moral Dilemmas: Comparing the Choices of Business and Law School Students. *Journal of Business Ethics* 10. 951-60.

McCabe, Donald L., Janet M. Dukerich and Jane E. Dutton (1994). The Effects of Professional Education on Values and the Resolution of Ethical Dilemmas: Business School vs. Law School Students. *Journal of Business Ethics* 13. 693-700.

McClintock, Charles G. (1972). Social Motivation – A Set of Propositions. *Behavioral Science* 17(5). 438-54.

Meier, Stephan and Alois Stutzer (2004). Is Volunteering Rewarding in Itself? Evidence from a Natural Experiment. *Working Paper.* University of Zurich.

Messick, David M. (1999). Alternative Logics for Decision Making in Social Settings. *Journal of Economic Behavior and Organization* 39(1). 11-28.

Moffitt, Robert A. (2001). Policy Intervention, Low-level Equilibria, and Social Interaction. In: Durlauf, Steven N. and Peyton H. Young (eds). *Social Dynamics.* Cambridge, MA: The MIT Press. 45-82.

Mueller, Dennis C. (2003). *Public Choice III.* Cambridge: Cambridge University Press.

Navarro, Peter (1988). Why Do Corporations Give to Charity? *Journal of Business* 61(1). 65-93.

Nyborg, Karine and Mari Rege (2003). Does Public Policy Crowd Out Private Contributions to Public Goods? *Public Choice* 115(3). 397-418.

Ockenfels, Axel and Joachim Weimann (1999). Types and Patterns: An Experimental East-West-German Comparison of Cooperation and Solidarity. *Journal of Public Economics* 71(2). 275-87.

O'Donoghue, Ted and Matthew Rabin (1999). Doing It Now or Later. *American Economic Review* 89(1). 103-24.

Offerman, Theo, Joep Sonnemans and Arthur Schram (1996). Value Orientations, Expectations and Voluntary Contributions in Public Goods. *Economic Journal* 106(437). 817-45.

Okten, Cagla and Burton A. Weisbrod (2000). Determinants of Donations in Private Nonprofit Markets. *Journal of Public Economics* 75(2). 255-72.

Oliner, S.P. and P.M. Oliner (1992). *The Altruistic Personality: Rescuers of Jews in Nazi Europe*. New York: Free Press.

Olson, Mancur (1965). *The Logic of Collective Action: Public Goods and the Theory of Groups*. Cambridge, MA: Harvard University Press.

Opp, Karl-Dieter (2001). Collective Political Action. *Analyse & Kritik* 23(1). 1-20.

Organ, Dennis W. and Katherine Ryan (1995). A Meta-analytic Review of Attitudinal and Dispositional Predictors of Organizational Citizenship Behavior. *Personnel Psychology* 48(4). 776-801.

Ortmann, Andreas and Gerd Gigerenzer (1997). Reasoning in Economics and Psychology: Why Social Context Matters. *Journal of Institutional and Theoretical Economics* 153(4). 700-710.

Ortmann, Andreas and Lisa K. Tichy (1999). Gender Differences in the Laboratory: Evidence from Prisoner's Dilemma Games. *Journal of Economic Behavior and Organization* 39(3). 327-39.

Osterloh, Margit and Bruno S. Frey (2000). Motivation, Knowledge Transfer and Organizational Forms. *Organization Science* 11(5). 538-50.

Osterloh, Margit, Sandra Rota and Bernhard Kuster (2003). Open Source Software Production: Climbing on the Shoulders of Giants. *Working Paper*. University of Zurich.

Ostrom, Elinor (1990). *Governing the Commons: The Evolution of Institutions for Collective Action*. Cambridge: Cambridge University Press.

Ostrom, Elinor (1998). A Behavioral Approach to the Rational Choice Theory of Collective Action. *American Political Science Review* 92(1). 1-22.

Ostrom, Elinor (2000). Collective Action and the Evolution of Social Norms. *Journal of Economic Perspectives* 14(3). 137-58.

Payne, Abigail (1998). Does the Government Crowd-out Private Donations? New Evidence from a Sample of Non-profit Firms. *Journal of Public Economics* 69(3). 323-45.

Pommerehne, Werner W. and Friedrich Schneider (1985). Politisch-ökonomische Überprüfung des Kaufkraftinzidenzkonzepts: Eine Analyse der AHV-Abstimmung von 1972 und 1978. In: Brugger, Ernst A. and René L. Frey (eds). *Sektorpolitik versus Regionalpolitik*. Diessenhofen: Rüegger. 75-100.

Potters, Jan, Martin Sefton and Lise Vesterlund (2005). After You – Endogenous Sequencing in Voluntary Contribution Games. *Journal of Public Economics* 89(8). 1399-419.

Rabin, Matthew (1993). Incorporating Fairness into Game Theory and Economics. *American Economic Review* 83(5). 1281-302.

Randolph, William C. (1995). Dynamic Income, Progressive Taxes, and the Timing of Charitable Contributions. *Journal of Political Economy* 103(4). 709-38.

Rege, Mari and Kjetil Telle (2004). The Impact of Social Approval and Framing on Cooperation in Public Good Situations. *Journal of Public Economics* 88(7-8). 1625-1644.

Reingen, P.H. (1982). Test of a List Procedure for Inducing Compliance with a Request to Donate Money. *Journal of Applied Psychology* 67(1). 110-18.

Ribar, David C. and Mark O. Wilhelm (2002). Altruistic and Joy of Giving Motivations in Charitable Behavior. *Journal of Political Economy* 110(2). 425-57.

Roberts, Russell D. (1984). A Positive Model of Private Charity and Public Transfers. *Journal of Political Economy* 92(1). 136-48.

Romano, Richard and Huseyin Yildirim (2001). Why Charities Announce Donations: A Positive Perspective. *Journal of Public Economics* 81(3). 423-47.

Ross, Lee, David Greene and Pamela House (1977). The 'False Consensus Effect': An Egocentric Bias in Social Perception and Attribution Processes. *Journal of Experimental Social Psychology* 13(3). 279-301.

Rotemberg, Julio (1994). Human Relations in the Workplace. *Journal of Political Economy* 102(4). 684-717.

Rotter, Julian B. (1966). Generalized Expectancies for Internal versus External Control of Reinforcement. *Psychological Monographs* 80(1). (whole no. 609).

Rousseau, Denise M. (1995). *Psychological Contracts in Organizations: Understanding Written and Unwritten Agreements*. Thousand Oaks, London and New Delhi: Sage Publications.

Ryan, Richard M., Kennon M. Sheldon, Tim Kasser and Edward L. Deci (1996). All Goals Are Not Created Equal: An Organismic Perspective on the Nature of Goals and Their Regulation. In: Gollwitzer, Peter M. and John A. Bargh (eds). *The Psychology of Action: Linking Cognition and Motivation to Behavior*. New York and London: Guilford Press. 7-26.

Sahlins, Marshall (1970). The Spirit of the Gift: Une Explication de Texte. In: Sahlins, Marshall (ed.). *Echanges et Communications, Mélanges offerts à Claude Lévi-Strauss à l'occasion de son 60e anniversaire*. Leiden: Mouton. 998-1011.

Sally, David (1995). Conversation and Cooperation in Social Dilemmas. A Meta-analysis of Experiments from 1958 to 1992. *Rationality and Society* 7(1). 58-92.

Sawyer, Jack (1966). The Altruism Scale: A Measure of Co-operative, Individualistic, and Competitive Interpersonal Orientation. *The American Journal of Sociology* 71(4). 407-16.

Schein, E. (1967). *Organization Psychology*. Englewood Cliffs, NJ: Prentice Hall.

Schelling, Thomas C. (1968). The Life You Save May Be Your Own. In: Chase, Samuel (ed.). *Problems in Public Expenditure Analysis*. Washington: Brookings Institute. 127-62.

Schooler, Jonathan W., Dan Ariely and George Loewenstein (2003). The Pursuit and Assessment of Happiness Can Be Self-defeating. In: Carillo, Juan D. and Isabelle Brocas (eds). *The Psychology of Economic Decisions. Volume I: Rationality and Well-being*. Oxford: Oxford University Press. 41-70.

Schram, Vicki R. and Marilyn M. Dunsing (1981). Influences on Married Women's Volunteer Work Participation. *Journal of Consumer Research* 7(4). 372-9.

Schroeder, David A., Thomas D. Jensen, Andrew J. Reed, Debra K. Sullivan and Michael Schwab (1983). The Actions of Others as Determinants of Behavior in a Social Trap Situation. *Journal of Experimental Social Psychology* 19. 522-39.

Schwarze, Johannes and Marco Härpfer (2005). Are People Inequality Averse, and Do They Prefer Redistribution by the State? Evidence From German Longitudinal Data on Life Satisfaction. *Journal of Socio-Economics*. Forthcoming.

Segal, Lewis M. and Burton Weisbrod (1998). Interdependence of Commercial and Donative Revenues. In: Weisbrod, Burton A. (ed.). *To Profit Or Not To Profit: The Commercial Transformation of the Nonprofit Sector*. Cambridge: Cambridge University Press. 105-27.

Seguino, Stephanie, Thomas Stevens and Mark A. Lutz (1996). Gender and Cooperative Behavior: Economic Man Rides Alone. *Feminist Economics* 2(1). 1-21.

Seligman, Clive, Joan Finegan, J. Douglas Hazelwood and Mark Wilkinson (1985). Manipulating Attributions for Profit: A Field Test of the Effects of Attributions on Behavior. *Social Cognition* 3(3). 313-21.

Selten, Reinhard and Axel Ockenfels (1998). An Experimental Solidarity Game. *Journal of Economic Behavior and Organization* 34(4). 517-39.

Shabman, Leonard and Kurt Stephenson (1994). A Critique of the Self-interested Voter Model: The Case of a Local Single Issue Referendum. *Journal of Economic Issues* 18(4). 1173-86.

Shang, Jen and Rachel Croson (2005). Field Experiments in Charitable Contribution: The Impact of Social Influence on the Voluntary Provision of Public Goods. *Working Paper*. University of Pennsylvania.

Simon, Herbert A. (1993). Altruism and Economics. *American Economic Review* 83(2). 156-61.

Slemrod, Joel (ed.) (1992). *Why People Pay Taxes. Tax Compliance and Enforcement.* Ann Arbor: University of Michigan Press.

Small, Deborah A. and George Loewenstein (2003). Helping the Victim or Helping *the* Victim: Altruism and Identifiability. *Journal of Risk and Uncertainty* 26(1). 5-16.

Smith, Adam (1759 [2000]). *The Theory of Moral Sentiments.* Amherst, New York: Prometheus Books.

Smith, Adam (1776 [1991]). *An Inquiry into the Nature and Causes of the Wealth of Nations.* Amherst, New York: Prometheus Books.

Smith, Kent W. (1992). Reciprocity and Fairness: Positive Incentives for Tax Compliance. In: Slemrod, Joel (ed.). *Why People Pay Taxes: Tax Compliance and Enforcement.* Ann Arbor: University of Michigan Press. 223-50.

Smith, Vincent H., Michael R. Kehoe and Mary E. Cremer (1995). The Private Provision of Public Goods: Altruism and Voluntary Giving. *Journal of Public Economics* 58(1). 107-26.

Sobel, Joel (2002). Can We Trust Social Capital? *Journal of Economic Literature* 40(1). 139-54.

Soetevent, Adriaan R. (2005). Anonymity in Giving in a Natural Context - An Economic Field Experiment in Thirty Churches. *Journal of Public Economics.* Forthcoming.

Sonnemans, Joep, Arthur Schram and Theo Offerman (1998). Public Good Provision and Public Bad Prevention: The Effect of Framing. *Journal of Economic Behavior and Organization* 34(1). 143-61.

Stanley, T.D. and Ume Tran (1998). Economics Students Need Not Be Greedy: Fairness and the Ultimatum Game. *Journal of Socio-Economics* 27(6). 657-64.

Steinberg, Richard (1991a). The Economics of Fund Raising. Burlingame, Dwight F. and Lamont J. Hulse (eds). *Taking Fund Raising Seriously.* San Francisco: Jossey-Bass. 239-56.

Steinberg, Richard S. (1991b). Does Government Spending Crowd Out Donations? Interpreting the Evidence. *Annals of Public and Cooperative Economics* 62(4). 591-617.

Stigler, George J. (1981). Economics or Ethics. In: McMurrin, S.M. (ed.). *Tanner Lectures on Human Values.* Cambridge: Cambridge University Press. 143-91.

Stigler, George J. (1984). Economics – The Imperial Science? *Scandinavian Journal of Economics* 86(3). 301-13.

Strotz, Robert H. (1956). Myopia and Inconsistency in Dynamic Utility Maximization. *Review of Economic Studies* 23. 165-80.

Stutzer, Alois and Bruno S. Frey (2003). Does Marriage Make People Happy, Or Do Happy People Get Married? *Journal of Socio-Economics.* Forthcoming.

Stutzer, Alois and Rafael Lalive (2004). The Role of Social Work Norms in Job Searching and Subjective Well-being. *Journal of the European Economic Association* 2(4). 696-719.

Sugden, Robert (1982). On the Economics of Philanthropy. *Economic Journal* 92. 341-50.

Sugden, Robert (1984). Reciprocity: The Supply of Public Goods Through Voluntary Contributions. *Economic Journal* 94(376). 772-87.

Tajfel, Henri (1981). *Human Groups and Social Categories Studies in Social Psychology.* London: Cambridge University Press.

Thaler, Richard H. and Cass R. Sunstein (2003). Libertarian Paternalism. *American Economic Review* 93(2). 175-9.

Throsby, David C. (1994). The Production and Consumption of the Arts: A View of Cultural Economics. *Journal of Economic Literature* 33(1). 1-29.

Titmuss, Richard M. (1970). *The Gift Relationship.* London: Allen & Unwin.

Trivers, Robert (1971). The Evolution of Reciprocal Altruism. *Quarterly Journal of Biology* 46. 32-57.

Tyran, Jean-Robert (2004). Voting When Money and Morals Conflict: An Experimental Test of Expressive Voting. *Journal of Public Economics* 88(7-8). 1645-64.

Tyran, Jean-Robert and Lars P. Feld (2002). Why People Obey the Law: Experimental Evidence from the Provision of Public Goods. *Working Paper.* CESIfo.

Unger, Lynette S. (1991). Altruism as a Motivation to Volunteer. *Journal of Economic Psychology* 12(1). 71-100.

van Lange, Paul A.M. (1992). Confidence in Expectations: A Test of the Triangle Hypothesis. *European Journal of Personality* 6(5). 371-9.

Varese, Federico and Meir Yaish (2000). The Importance of Being Asked: The Rescue of Jews in Nazi Europe. *Rationality and Society* 12(3). 307-34.

Vesterlund, Lise (2003). The Informational Value of Sequential Fundraising. *Journal of Public Economics* 87(3-4). 627-57.

Von Neumann, John and Oskar Morgenstern (1947). *Theory of Games and Economic Behavior.* Princeton: Princeton University Press.

Webley, Paul, Henry Robben and Ira Morris (1988). Social Comparison, Attitudes and Tax Evasion in a Shop Simulation. *Social Behaviour* 3(3). 219-28.

Weimann, Joachim (1994). Individual Behavior in a Free Riding Experiment. *Journal of Public Economics* 54(2). 185-200.

Wenzel, Michael (2001). Misperception of Social Norms About Tax Compliance: A Field-Experiment. *Working Paper*. Australian National University.

Wheeler, Judith A., Kevin M. Gorey and Bernard Greenblatt (1998). The Beneficial Effects of Volunteering for Older Volunteers and the People They Serve: A Meta-analysis. *International Journal of Aging and Human Development* 47(1). 69-79.

Wilson, John and Marc Musick (1999). The Effects of Volunteering on the Volunteer. *Law and Contemporary Problems* 62(4). 141-68.

Winkelmann, Liliana and Rainer Winkelmann (1998). Why Are the Unemployed So Unhappy? Evidence from Panel Data. *Economica* 65(257). 1-15.

Yezer, Anthony M., Robert S. Goldfarb and Paul J. Poppen (1996). Does Studying Economics Discourage Cooperation? Watch What We Do, Not What We Say or How We Play. *Journal of Economic Perspectives* 10(1). 177-86.

Index

age
  effect on pro-social behaviour 110
Akerlof, G. 21, 67
Albert, M. 24
Alesina, A. 28, 42, 67
Allison, S. 130
Alm, J. 10
altruism 18, 19, 20, 31, 38, 42, 43, 45,
  83, 102, 103
Amemiya, T. 70
Ames, R. 116
Andreoni, J. 10, 11, 13, 18, 19, 23, 24,
  26, 32, 33, 38, 74, 102, 103, 110,
  127
Anheier, H. 11
Argyle, M. 43
Aristotle 40
Ashforth, B. 66
Auten, G. 32

Ball, S. 56
Bardsley, N. 23
Becker, G. 12, 18
Beil, R. 116
belief management 95, 96, 139
Bénabou, R. 34
Benz, M. 37
bequest tax 32
Bertrand, M. 56
Besley, T. 37
Bierhoff, H.-W. 19
Bohnet, I. 11, 22, 23, 25, 26, 27, 29, 31,
  36, 95, 116
Bolton, G. 19, 64
Bosco, L. 23
Bowles, S. 21
Brandts, J. 24
Brennan, G. 27
Brown, E. 33
Buraschi, A. 15
business students

pro-social behaviour
  expectations of others' behaviour
    130, 134
  income factors 127, 128
  indoctrination hypothesis 123, 124,
    125, 126, 133
  perceived efficiency of fund
    management 129, 130
  selection hypothesis 121, 122, 130,
    131, 137–8
  see also economics students
Bütler, M. 11

Cadsby, C. 116
Camerer, C. 11, 12
Cameron, L. 58
Cardenas, J. C. 139
Carpenter, J. 28
Carter, J. 39, 116
Cech, P.-A. 56
Charness, G. 20
Cherry, T. 27, 127
Cialdini, R. 21, 22
civic duty 35, 36
  crowding-out by monetary incentives
    35–6
Clark, A. 42
Clotfelter, C. 39, 66, 82, 107, 110
Coleman, J. 27
Collard, D. 18
Collins, C. 32
common-pool resources
  use of 9, 11
communication 28, 29
competitors 38
conditional cooperation 22–4, 30, 45,
    46–7, 63, 64, 79, 82, 83, 87, 94, 95,
    96, 106, 136
  behavioural responses 86–7, 98
  belief management 95, 96
  composition of neighbourhoods 96

design of the field experiment 80–82,
        98
framing of information about
        behaviour of others 92–4
individual heterogeneity 88
law as a coordination device 96
measuring 79
motives 95
past behaviour, effect of 88, 89–92, 94
see also expectations of pro-social
        behaviour; reciprocity
Conlin, M. 21
Cookson, R. 26, 64
cooperators 38
Cooter, R. 26
Cornelli, F. 15
Cornes, R. 102
Croson, R. 23, 24, 82, 110
crowding-in effect of extrinsic incentives
        37
crowding-out 18, 19, 138
        matching donations 100, 103
        see also motivational crowding-out
Csikszentmihalyi, M. 43

Daboub, A. 114, 118
Davis, D. 99
Davis, L. 25
Dawes, R. 19, 21, 23, 67
Deci, E. 17, 34, 37, 100, 103
default settings 139
Di Tella, R. 42
Diekmann, A. 33, 58
Diener, E. 41
donations
        matching *see* matching donations
        methods of eliciting 2
Dunsing, M. 14

Earley, J. 40, 41, 44
Easterlin, R. 41
Eckel, C. 11, 18, 26, 59, 74, 99, 106,
        110
economics students
        pro-social behaviour 114, 118, 119,
                120, 131, 132, 137, 140
        expectations of others' behaviour
                130, 134
        field evidence 116–17
        income factors 127, 128

indoctrination hypothesis 117–18,
        123, 124, 125, 126, 131, 132,
        133, 138
laboratory experiments 115–16
perceived efficiency of fund
        management 129, 130
selection hypothesis 117, 120, 121,
        122, 130, 131, 137
survey studies 115
Economist 137
education
        influence on pro-social preferences
                39, 114
        see also business students; economics
                students
Eichenberger, R. 56
Elliott, C. 26, 64
ethics courses 131, 140
expectations of pro-social behaviour 79,
        84, 85
        belief management 95, 96, 139
        correlation with own behaviour 84,
                85, 90
        economics and business students 130,
                134

fairness 66, 83, 95, 139
Falk, A. 20, 21, 23, 95
false consensus effect 79, 85, 90
Farrel, J. 28
Fehr, E. 12, 20, 21, 29, 30, 36, 39, 58,
        61, 95, 104
Feld, L. 24
field experiments
        economics students' behaviour 116–17
        future research based on 47
        see also conditional cooperation;
                matching donations
Fischbacher, U. 20, 23, 38, 39, 62
Fleishman, J. 94
Fong, C. 21
framing effects 25, 26, 136, 139
        information about behaviour of others
                92–4
        ways of asking to contribute 64, 65,
                66, 76, 136
Frank, B. 116
Frank, R. 28, 39, 130
free-riders 1, 9, 10, 46
        mimicking the behaviour of 87

punishment of 21
Freeman, R. 29, 33
Frey, B. 9, 11, 12, 17, 21, 22, 25, 26, 27, 29, 31, 32, 34, 35, 37, 39, 40, 41, 42, 66, 100, 103, 116, 132, 139
fringe benefits 14, 15, 16
Fudenberg, D. 16
fundraising *see* donations

Gächter, S. 20, 21, 27, 30, 61, 95
Gandal, N. 115
Gates, W. 32
gender differences in pro-social behaviour 109, 110
    relative price effect 110, 111, 113
German Socio-Economic Panel (GSOEP) 44
Ghatak, M. 37
Gigerenzer, G. 130
Glaeser, E. 83, 88
Glazer, A. 14, 15
Gneezy, U. 35, 103, 110
Goldstein, N. 22
Götte, L. 35
Gouldner, A. 21
Greene, W. 34, 73
Grossman, P. 11, 18, 26, 59, 74, 99, 106, 110
group identification
    influence on pro-social behaviour 2, 28, 66–8
Gruber, J. 42
GSOEP 44

happiness *see* utility
Harbaugh, W. 14, 15
Hardin, G. 9
Härpfer, M. 43
Harris, M. 44
Haucap, J. 132
Hayward, D. 64
Heldt, T. 24
Henrich, J. 11, 26
heterogeneity
    conditional cooperation 88
    pro-social preferences 38–9
    social comparison 83
Hoffman, E. 22, 25, 28, 61
Houser, D. 62

identifiable victims 26
in-group effects *see* group identification
individual heterogeneity *see* heterogeneity
individualists 38
inequality aversion 20
    increasing utility 42, 43
institutional environment 25, 26, 29, 31, 39, 45, 46, 47
    framing effects 25, 26, 64, 65, 66, 76, 92–4, 136, 139
    see also communication; group identification; property rights
intrinsic motivation 17, 31, 46
    crowding-in effect of extrinsic incentives 37
    see also motivational crowding-out
Iran
    earthquake aid 1
Irons, M. 39, 116
Isaac, R. 25, 64
Isen, A. 44

Jegen, R. 34
Johannesson, M. 22, 25, 61
Jones, T. 117
Just, T. 132

Kahan, D. 95
Kahneman, D. 41
Kandinsky, W. 28
Kaplan, S. 23
Kasser, T. 41
Katok, E. 19
Kelley, H. 38
Kelman, S. 114
Keser, C. 24
Kingma, B. 18
Kirchgässner, G. 127
Klee, P. 28
Kollock, P. 28
Kolm, S.-C. 21
Konow, J. 12, 26, 28, 40, 41, 44
Konrad, K. 14, 15
Kranton, R. 67
Kreps, D. 16
Kurzban, R. 24, 62, 95

La Ferrara, E. 28, 67
Laband, D. 116

Laibson, D. 66
Lalive, R. 42
Lankford, H. 33
Lazear, E. 12, 37
Ledyard, J. 11, 21, 110
Lepper, M. 34
Levi, M. 10
Levin, P. 44
Liebrand, W. 38
Lindenberg, S. 64
List, J. 24, 36, 107
Loewenstein, G. 27, 41
Long, S. 29
Lucking-Reiley, D. 24, 107
Ludwig, J. 96
Luttmer, E. 28, 67

Mael, F. 66
Marks, G. 23
Marwell, G. 116
Maskin, E. 16
matching donations 32, 99, 100, 139–40
    behavioural hypotheses 102, 103, 104
    crowding-out effect 100, 103
    design of field experiment 100–102
    impact of 104, 105, 106, 107, 110,
        111, 112, 113, 136–7
        gender effect 109, 110, 113
        pro-socially inclined people 108,
            109, 111
        selfish people 107, 108, 111
    motivational crowding-out effect 100,
        103, 112
    see also relative price effect
Maynes, E. 116
MBAs 114
    see also business students
McCabe, D. 115, 131
McClintock, C. 38
Messick, D. 22
Miller, J. 18, 33, 38
Miller, N. 23
Mittone, L. 23
Moffitt, R. 96
monetary incentives 31, 32, 99
    see also matching donations; relative
        price effect; taxes
Morgenstern, O. 117
motivational crowding-out 34, 35, 36,
    37, 38, 137, 138, 139

civic duty 35–6
    matching donations 100, 103, 112
Mueller, D. 11
Mullainathan, S. 42, 56
Musick, M. 43

neighbourhoods, composition of 96
North, D. 25
Nyborg, K. 13

Oberholzer-Gee, F. 35, 56, 139
Ockenfels, A. 23, 130
O'Donohue, T. 66
Offerman, T. 24
Olson, M. 14, 15
Opp, K.-D. 29
opportunity costs 33
Organ, D. 66
Ortmann, A. 74, 130
Osterloh, M. 11
Ostrom, E. 11, 25, 29, 30, 114
Oswald, A. 42

Payne, A. 19
Persson, B. 22, 25, 61
Pettit, P. 27
politicians
    incentives of 96
Pommerehne, W. 11
Potters, J. 23, 95
Preisendörfer, P. 58
prestige motive 14, 15, 16, 103
price elasticities 32, 33, 34
    see also relative price effect
pro-social behaviour 2, 135, 138
    extent of 11
    motivations for
        heterogeneity of preferences 38–9
        importance of understanding 12–13
        intrinsic motivation 17, 31, 46
        pro-social preferences theories
            17–20, 45
        selective incentives 14, 15, 16
        see also institutional environment;
            monetary incentives;
            reciprocity; utility
property rights 27, 28
public goods
    provision of 9–10
        suboptimal outcomes 10

signals of quality of 22–3, 83, 95, 106
tax financing of 10
see also pro-social behaviour
public policy 138, 139
see also crowding-out
punishment of free-riders 21

Rabin, M. 20, 28, 66
Randolph, W. 32
rebates *see* taxes
reciprocity 1, 2, 20–22, 30, 45, 46, 106
see also conditional cooperation
Reckers, P. 23
Rege, M. 13, 27
Reingen, P. 25
relative price effect 32, 33, 34, 47, 102
gender differences 110, 111, 113
substitutes and complements 33
see also matching donations;
motivational crowding-out; taxes
'rent leavers' 11
Ribar, D. 18, 19
Riedl, A. 27
Roberts, R. 18, 103
Roccas, S. 115
Romano, R. 23
Rondeau, D. 107
Ross, L. 23, 79
Rotemberg, J. 18
Rotter, J. 37
Rustichini, A. 35, 103
Ryan, R. 41, 66, 100, 103

Sahlins, M. 21
Salamon, L. 11
Sally, D. 28
Samuelson, L. 24
Sandler, T. 102
Sausgruber, R. 23
Sawyer, J. 115
Schein, E. 115
Schelling, T. 26
Schmidt, K. 12, 20, 29, 104
Schneider, F. 11
Scholz, J. 24
Schooler, J. 41
Schram, V. 14, 24
Schroeder, D. 23
Schulze, G. 116
Schwarze, J. 43

'seed money' 24–5
Seguino, S. 116
selective incentives 14, 15, 16
self-control problems 66
self-determination 37
self-interest 1, 9, 10, 11, 12, 13, 16, 138
Seligman, C. 21
Selten, R. 23, 130
Shabman, L. 11
Shang, J. 24
signals of quality of public goods 22–3,
83, 95, 106
Simon, H. 67
Slemrod, J. 10
Smith, A. 9, 16, 40
Smith, K. 21
Smith, R. 44
Smith, V. 18
Sobel, J. 25
social comparison 22–3, 24, 45, 46–7,
79
heterogeneity 83
see also conditional cooperation;
reciprocity; signals of quality of
public goods; social norms
social interaction 2, 3, 136, 138, 139
social norms 22, 83, 95
Soetevent, A. 27
Sonnemans, J. 26, 64
Spitzer, M. 28
sponsor-specific recipients 26
Stahelski, A. 38
Stanley, T. 116
state intervention 138, 139
see also crowding-out
Steinberg, R. 13
Stephenson, K. 11
Stigler, G. 12
Strotz, R. 66
Stutzer, A. 40, 41, 42, 44
subjective well-being *see* utility
subsidizing pro-social behaviour 31, 32,
99
see also matching donations; relative
price effect; taxes
Sugden, R. 18, 20
Sunstein, C. 139
Switzerland
donations to victims of landslide 2
see also University of Zurich

Tajfel, H. 28
taxes
  bequest tax 32
  compliance 10, 23, 24, 36
  financing public goods 10
  incentives for donations 31–2, 99, 100
  system reform 139
Telle, K. 27
Thaler, R. 11, 19, 21, 23, 67, 139
Throsby, D. 9
Tichy, L. 74
Tirole, J. 34
Titmuss, R. 34
Tran, U. 116
Trivers, R. 27
trust-based pro-social behaviour 36
  effect of extrinsic incentives 36, 37
Tyran, J.-R. 24

Unger, L. 18
University of Zurich
  students' contributions to social funds
      54, 69–70
    conditional cooperation 63, 64
    data set 53, 54–5, 56–9
    different disciplines, influence of
        70, 71, 72, 77, 78
    feedback concerning behaviour of
        others 62, 63, 76
    freshmen, contribution rates of 68,
        69
    level of contributions 59, 60
    on-line survey 56, 58, 126
    past behaviour 59, 60, 61, 78
    repetition of the decision to
        contribute, effect of 61, 62, 76
    students' awareness of others'
        behaviour 63

  see also business students; conditional
      cooperation; economics students;
      institutional environment;
      matching donations
utility
  effect of pro-social behaviour 40,
      42–5
  influences on 41–2
  measurement of 40, 41

van Winden, F. 24
Varese, F. 29
Vesterlund, L. 23, 74, 95, 107, 110
volunteering
  effect on happiness 43–5
  monetary incentives reducing
      motivation 35
Von Neumann, J. 117
voting 10–11

'warm glow' motive 19, 31, 43,
    102–3
Webley, P. 23
Weimann, J. 87
well-being *see* utility
Wenzel, M. 24, 85
Wheeler, J. 43
Wilhelm, M. 18, 19
Wilson, J. 43
Winkelmann, L. 42
Winkelmann, R. 42

Yaish, M. 29
Yezer, A. 116, 130
Yildirim, H. 23

Zeckhauser, R. 23, 95
Zurich *see* University of Zurich